The Doberman Pinscher

OUR BEST FRIENDS

Adopting a Pet

The Beagle

The Boston Terrier

The Boxer

The Bulldog

Caring for Your Mutt

The Chihuahua

The Cocker Spaniel

The Dachshund

The Doberman Pinscher

Ferrets

Fetch this Book

Gerbils

The German Shepherd

The Golden Retriever

Guinea Pigs

Hamsters

The Labrador Retriever

Lizards

The Miniature Schnauzer

Mixed Breed Cats

The Pomeranian

The Poodle

The Pug

Rabbits

The Rottweiler

The Shih Tzu

Snakes

Turtles

The Yorkshire Terrier

OUR BEST FRIENDS

The Doberman Pinscher

September Morn

ELDORADO INK

Produced by OTTN Publishing, Stockton, New Jersey

Eldorado Ink
PO Box 100097
Pittsburgh, PA 15233
www.eldoradoink.com

CPSIA compliance information: Batch#OBF010111-5. For further information,
contact Eldorado Ink at info@eldoradoink.com.

First printing

1 3 5 7 9 8 6 4 2

Library of Congress Cataloging-in-Publication Data

Morn, September B.
    The Doberman pinscher / September Morn.
        p. cm. — (Our best friends)
    Includes bibliographical references and index.
    ISBN 978-1-932904-77-2 (hardcover) — ISBN 978-1-932904-83-3 (trade)
    1. Doberman pinscher . I. Title.
    SF429.D6M67 2011
    636.73'6—dc22

                                        2010034479

Photo credits: © American Animal Hospital Association, 52; courtesy Delta Society: 75;
© Cynoclub/iStockphoto.com: 89; © Melanie DeFazio/iStockphoto.com: 44; © Javier Escriva
Dura/iStockphoto.com: 98; © Cass Greene/iStockphoto.com: 47; © Majoros Laszlo/iStock
photo.com: 81; © Gary Martin/iStockphoto.com: 79; © Brianna May/iStockphoto.com: 95;
© Jupiter Images: 27; Library of Congress: 19; courtesy Pet Sitters International: 90; used under
license from Shutterstock, Inc., 3, 8, 10, 11, 12, 13, 14, 16, 20, 21, 22, 23, 25, 29, 30, 31, 32,
33, 38, 39, 40, 41, 42, 46, 51, 53, 55, 57, 58, 61, 63, 64, 65, 69, 70, 71, 72, 76, 77, 78, 83, 86,
87, 92, 93, 94, 96, 97, 108, front cover (all), back cover; U.S. Department of Defense: 18.

**For information about custom editions, special sales, or premiums,
please contact our special sales department at info@eldoradoink.com.**

TABLE OF CONTENTS

Introduction by Gary Korsgaard, DVM   6

1   Is a Doberman Pinscher Right for You?   9

2   Breed History and Background   16

3   Responsible Pet Ownership   22

4   Finding the Right Doberman   30

5   Caring for Your Puppy (Birth to Six Months)   38

6   Your Doberman's Health   51

7   Things to Know as Your Puppy Grows   65

8   Training Your Doberman Pinscher   76

9   Caring for Your Senior Doberman Pinscher   92

Organizations to Contact   100
Further Reading   104
Internet Resources   105
Index   107
Contributors   112

Introduction

GARY KORSGAARD, DVM

The mutually beneficial relationship between humans and animals began long before the dawn of recorded history. Archaeologists believe that humans began to capture and tame wild goats, sheep, and pigs more than 9,000 years ago. These animals were then bred for specific purposes, such as providing humans with a reliable source of food or providing furs and hides that could be used for clothing or the construction of dwellings.

Other animals had been sought for companionship and assistance even earlier. The dog, believed to be the first animal domesticated, began living and working with Stone Age humans in Europe more than 14,000 years ago. Some archaeologists believe that wild dogs and humans were drawn together because both hunted the same prey. By taming and training dogs, humans became more effective hunters. Dogs, meanwhile, enjoyed the social contact with humans and benefited from greater access to food and warm shelter. Dogs soon became beloved pets as well as trusted workers. This can be seen from the many artifacts depicting dogs that have been found at ancient sites in Asia, Europe, North America, and the Middle East.

The earliest domestic cats appeared in the Middle East about 5,000 years ago. Small wild cats were probably first attracted to human settlements because plenty of rodents could be found wherever harvested grain was stored. Cats played a useful role in hunting and killing these pests, and it is likely that grateful humans rewarded them for this assistance. Over time, these small cats gave up some of their aggressive wild behaviors and began living among humans. Cats eventually became so popular in ancient Egypt that they were believed to possess magical powers. Cat statues were placed outside homes to ward off evil spirits, and mummified cats were included in royal tombs to accompany their owners into the afterlife.

Today, few people believe that cats have supernatural powers, but most pet owners feel a magical bond with their pets, whether they are dogs, cats, hamsters, rabbits, horses, or parrots. The lives of pets and their people become inextricably intertwined, providing strong emotional and physical rewards for both humans and animals. People of all ages can benefit from the loving companionship of a pet. Not surprisingly, then, pet ownership is widespread. Recent statistics indicate that about 60 percent of all households in the United States and Canada have at least one pet, while the figure is close to 50 percent of households in the United Kingdom. For millions of people, therefore, pets truly have become their "best friends."

Finding the best animal friend can be a challenge, however. Not only are there many types of domesticated pets, but each has specific needs, characteristics, and personality traits. Even within a category of pets, such as dogs, different breeds will flourish in different surroundings and with different treatment. For example, a German Shepherd may not be the right pet for a person living in a cramped urban apartment; that person might be better off caring for a smaller dog like a Toy Poodle or Shih Tzu, or perhaps a cat. On the other hand, an active person who loves the outdoors may prefer the companionship of a Labrador Retriever to that of a small dog or a passive indoor pet like a goldfish or hamster.

The joys of pet ownership come with certain responsibilities. Bringing a pet into your home and your neighborhood obligates you to care for and train the pet properly. For example, a dog must be housebroken, taught to obey your commands, and trained to behave appropriately when he encounters other people or animals. Owners must also be mindful of their pet's particular nutritional and medical needs.

The purpose of the OUR BEST FRIENDS series is to provide a helpful and comprehensive introduction to pet ownership. Each book contains the basic information a prospective pet owner needs in order to choose the right pet for his or her situation and to care for that pet throughout the pet's lifetime. Training, socialization, proper nutrition, potential medical issues, and the legal responsibilities of pet ownership are thoroughly explained and discussed, and an abundance of expert tips and suggestions are offered. Whether it is a hamster, corn snake, guinea pig, or Labrador Retriever, the books in the OUR BEST FRIENDS series provide everything the reader needs to know about how to have a happy, well-adjusted, and well-behaved pet.

Doberman Pinschers are known to be intelligent, alert, and loyal. These sleek and agile dogs make great pets and companions. As a result, since 2005 they have been ranked among the 20 most popular dog breeds in the United States.

CHAPTER ONE

Is a Doberman Pinscher Right for You?

The Doberman Pinscher breed was developed to work with and protect humans. They are natural guards that are ready and willing to defend members of their human family from any perceived danger. These sleek and muscular dogs are also exceptional athletes and can excel at almost any canine sport. When raised and socialized properly, Dobes make gentle, polite, and devoted companions that appreciate being included in the activities of their human family. Due to their versatile intelligence, loyal courage, and handsome physique, it is not surprising that Doberman Pinschers have become very popular in the United States and elsewhere around the world.

A member of the Working group of dog breeds, Doberman Pinschers are very trainable. Dobermans learn quickly and have an excellent memory. These dogs enjoy performing tasks and tricks that make them feel useful and appreciated. Even small jobs, like fetching his leash before walks or returning his empty bowl after dinner, will give your Doberman a sense of duty and pride. With their genetic heritage as guard dogs, a Doberman Pinscher will often take up a sentry position where he can guard the home and family.

Doberman Pinschers need daily physical and mental exercise to stay healthy and well behaved. Without a regular outlet for their high energy and intelligence, Dobermans can become distressed and destructive. A bored Doberman may take on duties that you don't want them to—such as "guarding" neighboring homes from their owners, and barking loudly whenever they approach. This kind of bored-Doberman job can lose friends for the dogs' owners and may invite embarrassing visits from animal control officials. To live happily with a Doberman Pinscher, you will need to train him to behave in appropriate ways.

If you treasure the devoted companionship of a loyal, handsome, large, strong dog, and enjoy training and interacting with a highly intelligent canine pal, then a Doberman Pinscher could be the perfect match for you.

ROLES FOR YOUR DOBERMAN PINSCHER

Doberman Pinschers make excellent pets and companions because they form deep bonds of loyalty with their humans. These dogs will enjoy spending time with you and being part of the family. Beyond simple companionship, you and your

With proper training and care, Doberman Pinschers can make great family pets.

Doberman Pinscher may enjoy participating together in competitive sports like Agility, Obedience, Rally, Tracking, or Conformation. If you teach a Doberman Pinscher what you want him to do, he will try his best to fulfill whatever role you require.

Dobermans are among the most intelligent, perceptive, and intuitive dog breeds. They are often able to sense danger even before an actual threat has occurred, and will move into a position to protect the owner. As a result, these dogs excel at police work and in military service. They fulfill many civilian roles as well. Doberman Pinschers serve admirably as Service Dogs, helping physically disabled humans, as well as emotional therapy dogs.

Whatever task you have in mind for your dog—whether it is as a therapeutic visitation dog, a show ring competitor, a full-time buddy, a search-and-rescue partner, or a watchful home protector—a Doberman Pinscher can do the job, and do it well.

THE BEST ENVIRONMENT FOR THE BREED

Doberman Pinschers were originally bred to guard and protect their owners. Generations of careful selective breeding have gentled the Doberman

Doberman Pinschers combine intelligence with natural athletic ability, making them very successful in competitive dog sports and skilled at police work.

temperament to make it a trustworthy family companion. Doberman Pinschers have a deep-seated need to interact closely with their human owner and her family. In any type of home environment, good training will help a Doberman Pinscher understand his owner's expectations and how to behave appropriately. Not even the most brilliant Doberman is born knowing all the rules. The Doberman requires a calm, firm, and

TAIL DOCKING AND EAR CROPPING

According to the American Kennel Club's breed standard, a description of the ideal characteristics for Doberman Pinschers, the dogs' tails should be amputated at the second tail vertebrae. This procedure is performed when a puppy is only a couple days old, so it will have been done well before you acquire a purebred dog from a breeder.

Historically, the tails of working dogs like Dobermans were docked for practical purposes. A working dog's tail can become injured, and this damage does not heal easily and can eventually affect a dog's overall health. However, tail docking is painful for the dog, so today some American breeders opt not to perform this procedure on their puppies. Germany and several other European countries have outlawed tail docking, so Doberman Pinschers in those places possess natural tails. A Doberman is aesthetically pleasing even without a docked tail.

Working dogs like Dobermans often had their ears cropped as well. This procedure involves cutting away part of the ear, then bandaging the ears so that cartilage grows in a way that makes the ear stand up straight. There were two reasons for cropping. Since these were guard dogs, cropping the ears provided fewer sensitive areas for a potential attacker to grab. Second, cutting away the fold of skin over a Doberman's ear makes it easier for him to identify where sounds are coming from. Typically, cropping is done when a Doberman is between seven and nine weeks old; waiting longer runs the risk that the ear cartilage will already have developed improperly.

Because ear cropping does cause pain to the dog, and does carry some medical risks, today some breeders are opting not to perform this procedure on their puppies. The AKC breed standard for Doberman Pinschers says that ears should be "normally cropped and carried erect." However, there is no deduction for uncropped ears in AKC Conformation events, although uncropped Doberman Pinschers remain relatively rare in the show ring.

A Doberman's ears must be taped after they are cropped so that they stand up properly.

stable owner who will teach him good manners and gentle behavior, beginning when he's a puppy.

Dobermans need exercise and mental stimulation every day. They are high-energy dogs that require long walks and vigorous free exercise like swimming or games of fetch. After their need for mental and physical exercise has been met, most Doberman Pinschers are able to settle comfortably and relax with their families.

The Doberman Pinscher is a versatile dog, both in the type of work he can do and the type of environment in which he can live. A Doberman can be equally content living on a ranch or in an urban townhouse, as long as he has proper exercise for his body, a useful job or task to satisfy his mind, and a person to accompany, love, and protect.

COSTS INVOLVED BEYOND THE PURCHASE PRICE

Regardless of whether you obtain your Doberman Pinscher as a gift or pay two months' wages for him, that initial price is just the beginning of what your dog will cost. The price of maintaining a dog will vary, depending on his age, health, the cost of food and veterinary services where you live, and the lifestyle you choose for your Doberman. Here is a basic

Some people make the mistake of thinking a dog with a strong personality will help them gain the confidence and assertiveness they lack, only to find out that such a dog is too much for them to handle. The truth is that an assertive, confident dog like a Doberman Pinscher requires an assertive, confident owner!

list of the approximate costs necessary to maintain a Doberman Pinscher for a year. Keep in mind that as the cost of living changes, so does the cost of owning a dog.

Balls and sturdy chew toys will help keep your Doberman puppy entertained.

FOOD: $350 to $1,800, depending on what type of food you feed your Doberman. Foods with better-quality ingredients typically cost more, but "cheap" dog food is often no bargain, because the better-quality foods are more nourishing, more palatable, easier to digest, and more beneficial to the dog's overall health.

VETERINARY CARE: $250 to $800. These costs reflect the price of well-dog care, including veterinary exams, immunizations, and protection from heartworm, fleas, ticks, and other parasites. Illnesses, accidents, or injuries will quickly increase this expense by hundreds or thousands of dollars.

FAST FACT

When a Doberman Pinscher makes friends with a person, he will remember that person when they meet again.

TRAINING: $200 to $900 for the first few years of your Doberman's life. Training costs vary widely, depending on whether you take private or group lessons and what kind of training you're doing with your Dobe. Basic manners classes are the bare minimum. To fully enjoy your Doberman Pinscher, continue training beyond the basic skills and develop your dog's inherent talents.

GROOMING: $75 to $850, depending on whether you bathe and groom your Doberman Pinscher yourself or hire a groomer to perform these tasks. The high-end estimate is based on one professional grooming per month.

EVERYDAY ESSENTIALS: $200 to $1,200. This category includes such

FAST FACT

Training is an essential component of responsible dog ownership. People don't appreciate dogs that jump all over them, knock their children down, bark or howl incessantly, or destroy their property. When you teach your dog not to do these things at home, your dog will display good manners in public as well.

everyday items as collars, leashes, food dishes, chew toys, beds, and bedding.

These basic costs add up to a minimum of $1,075 a year, but they could go much higher, depending on the cost of living in your area and how much your family wants to pamper your Doberman Pinscher.

CHAPTER TWO

Breed History and Background

The Doberman Pinscher breed originated in Germany between the 1860s and the 1890s. Karl Friedrich Louis Dobermann, a tax collector and dogcatcher in Apolda, a town in central Germany, originally developed the breed. At the time, collecting taxes involved travel around the countryside, and there was always a danger that bandits might try to rob the collector. Dobermann wanted a dog that would be a good companion and protector when he was on his official duties.

The exact mix of breeds that contributed to the genetic makeup of the Doberman Pinscher is not definitively known. Because he ran the Apolda dog pound, Karl Dobermann had access to many kinds of dogs.

The first Doberman Pinschers were bred in Apolda, Germany, during the late 19th century.

Some of the dogs that contributed to the Doberman breed probably included Rottweilers, Black and Tan Terriers, German Pinschers, and shorthaired shepherd-type dogs. In 1863, Dobermann began selling the puppies that resulted from his breeding attempts. They proved to be very popular, and he continued trying to improve the breed over the next three decades.

In 1890, the German Kennel Club adopted a breed standard for the dogs, which were named Dobermann Pinschers in honor of their founder. After Karl Louis Dobermann's death in 1894, other breeders took up the task. A friend named Otto Goeller continued with the breeding program and founded the National Dobermann Pinscher Club in 1899. Another notable early breeder was Goswin Tischler, who introduced characteristics of Greyhounds and Manchester Terriers into the breed.

In the early 20th century, the Doberman Pinscher breed spread to the United Kingdom and the United States. The American Kennel Club (AKC) recognized the Doberman Pinscher breed in 1908, placing it into the Working Group. Since that time, Dobermans have been eligible to compete in AKC events and shows.

FAST FACT

In Germany today, a dog of this breed is referred to as a Dobermann; the word "pinscher" was dropped from the German name during the 1940s, because in Germany pinschers are terrier-type dogs bred to hunt rats and other small mammals. In the United Kingdom, the dogs are also referred to as Dobermanns, while in the United States and Canada the accepted name is Doberman Pinscher.

BREED STANDARD

Each breed of purebred dog has a parent club, which is organized and led by experienced breeders and other fanciers of that breed. Each parent club develops a written description of the perfect dog of that breed, and this is the criterion by which dogs of that breed are judged in the show ring. This description is known as the Standard of Perfection, or the breed standard. The Standard of Perfection always covers the proper appearance and gait, and many standards also include a description of the ideal temperament of the breed. Reputable breeders strive to produce dogs that conform to the Standard of Perfection as closely as possible.

The Doberman Pinscher Club of America (DPCA), a nonprofit organization, is the parent organization for the breed in the United States. The DPCA is a member of the American Kennel Club, and the AKC posts the

DOGS OF WAR

During World War II, Doberman Pinschers were highly regarded for military work. The United States Marine Corps's first war dog platoon worked with Doberman Pinschers. Marine dog/handler teams walked "point" on Guadalcanal and other Pacific islands, venturing into enemy territory ahead of the troops and checking the territory for snipers, ambushes, and mines. Close teamwork and communication between the handlers and their highly trained Doberman Pinschers uncovered dangers and prevented many American casualties. War dogs also served as sentries and messengers.

At the U.S. Naval Station in Guam, the war dog memorial, "Always Faithful," depicts an alert Doberman Pinscher. The statue honors the 25 dogs that were killed while helping U.S. Marines liberate the island from the Japanese in 1944. The memorial also represents the hundreds of heroic dogs that served with the Marine Corps during World War II.

(Left) Marine dog handlers patrol the South Pacific island of Bougainville, December 1943. (Above) A statue of a Doberman Pinscher sits atop the U.S. Marine Corps war dog memorial on Guam.

official breed standard developed by the club on its Web site, at http://www.akc.org/breeds/doberman_pinscher/index.cfm. The breed standards formulated by Doberman clubs in Canada and the United Kingdom are very similar to the U.S. standard.

The Doberman Pinscher breed standard describes the breed in detail, but even a finely detailed description leaves some room for interpretation by individual breeders. However, all reputable Doberman Pinscher breeders work to uphold the breed standard through their breeding programs and practices.

Doberman Pinschers that don't adhere to the breed standard can still make wonderful pets and companions. However, if you plan to enter your canine friend in dog shows, he'll need to match the AKC specifications as closely as possible. Dogs

Philadelphia socialite George H. Earle III founded the Doberman Pinscher Club of America in 1921. Earle would later serve as governor of Pennsylvania from 1935 to 1939.

that don't conform to the breed standard will be disqualified from AKC-sanctioned Conformation shows. In addition, for obvious reasons, they are not good dogs to use for breeding prospective champions.

APPEARANCE AND CHARACTERISTICS

According to the AKC breed standard, purebred Doberman Pinschers should appear tall and elegant. Their athletic ability is apparent from the graceful ways that they move. Males

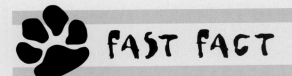

FAST FACT

In 1939, a Doberman Pinscher named Ch. Ferry v Raufelsen won Best in Show at the Westminster Kennel Club Dog Show. It was the first time a Doberman won the prestigious annual event. Since then, a Doberman has won three other times, most recently in 1989.

Black with rust-colored markings, as shown above, is the most common coat color among Doberman Pinschers. Fawn coats like the one below are the rarest coloring for purebred Dobermans.

are 26 to 28 inches (66–71 cm) tall at the withers (front shoulders), while females should be 24 to 26 inches (61–66 cm). According to the American Kennel Club's breed standard, the ideal height for a male dog is 27.5 inches (70 cm), and for a female is 25.5 inches (65 cm). Male Dobermans generally weigh between 75 and 100 pounds (34–45 kg), while females weigh 60 to 90 pounds (27–41 kg).

A purebred Doberman Pinscher will have a squarish shape when viewed from the side. His height at the withers will be the same as his length measured horizontally from the forechest to the rear projection of the upper thigh. The Doberman's head, neck, and legs should be in proportion to the length and depth of his body. The natural tail is long and tapers to a point. However, it is common for these dogs' tails to be docked, or cut short, when they are just a few days old.

The Doberman's short, sleek coat comes in several colors: black, red, blue, or fawn (a light brown). In purebred dogs, all of these colors will include clearly defined rust-colored markings above the eyes; on the muzzle, throat, and forechest; on the legs and feet; and below the tail. Some Dobermans may have a small white patch (ideally, not more than half an inch square) on their chest.

A Doberman Pinscher's long head can be said to resemble a blunt wedge. When seen from the front, the head should widen gradually toward the base of the ears in a practically unbroken line. A Doberman's eyes are almond-shaped and set moderately deep in the head. These

FAST FACT

White is not a permitted coat color for purebred Doberman Pinschers. Albino Dobes tend to inherit genetic problems with their eyes and their skin.

dogs' ears are located at the top of the skull. They are normally cropped when the Doberman is a puppy, and carried erect. If left uncropped, the ears will be folded forward when the dog is at alert. The nose should be black on black-coated Dobermans, dark brown on dogs with a red coat, dark gray on blue-coated Dobes, and dark tan on fawn Dobermans.

Although the American breed standard calls for the ears of a purebred Doberman Pinscher to be cropped, in recent years some breeders have opted to skip this surgical procedure. This brown-coated Doberman puppy sports uncropped ears.

CHAPTER THREE

Responsible Pet Ownership

As the owner of a Doberman Pinscher, you are morally responsible for his care and training. You are also legally responsible for any damage or injury your dog might cause. Each state, county, and municipality has its own rules related to dog ownership, so take time to learn about the laws where you live.

Owning a powerful, protective dog like a Doberman Pinscher means you may encounter legal issues that owners of smaller breeds do not. Some communities have passed laws banning certain large and medium-sized dog breeds, such as Dobermans, Rottweilers, pit bulls, and German Shepherds. In other communities, breed-specific laws

Your Doberman Pinscher should always wear an ID tag, in case he becomes lost.

impose strict restrictions on the owners of such dogs. These might include requiring owners to purchase special licenses, to buy liability insurance, to keep their dogs behind six-foot-high fences, or to muzzle their dogs in public. Know the laws and regulations in your home area and the places you might travel to with your dog, so you and your Doberman stay legal and free.

One type of rule almost every urban and suburban community enforces is the licensing of dogs. Licensing costs can vary considerably, but almost all communities charge less—often significantly less—to license a spayed or neutered dog than an intact one. If an unlicensed dog is picked up as a stray, his owner may have to pay a steep fine for failing to comply with licensing laws, plus the cost of buying a license. The best approach is to abide by all licensing requirements in your area.

When you're walking in a public area, it's best to keep your Doberman Pinscher on a sturdy leash. You want to protect others from possible aggression by your dog, and protect your Dobe from traffic or other dangerous situations.

Another issue that a dog owner must take seriously is preventing her dog from biting. According to the Centers for Disease Control in Atlanta, dogs bite about 4.7 million people in the United States every year. Of those bite victims, about 800,000 require some form of medical attention. Though Doberman Pinschers are usually friendly, any dog will bite if he feels threatened or cornered. Keep your dog safe and out of trouble by training him properly and keeping him under control when you take him out in public.

IDENTIFICATION

Proper identification on your dog is important for his safety, as well as for your own peace of mind. If your Doberman Pinscher were ever lost or stolen, good ID could be the key to getting him back. The three most common types of ID are collar tags, tattoos, and microchip implants. There are pluses and minuses to each of these identification methods, so it's a good idea to equip your dog with more than one type of ID.

COLLAR TAGS: A plastic or metal ID tag fastened to your Doberman's collar, with your contact information engraved on it, is a good first line of defense. Anyone finding your dog can easily read the tag and contact

FAST FACT

Dogs have worn collars for thousands of years, for adornment and identification as well as for control.

you directly. For security reasons you may not choose to list your name, your dog's name, or your home address on the tag, but the tag should include at least your home and cell phone numbers and perhaps your e-mail address. It's also worthwhile to include your city and state of residence on the tag, so the person who finds your lost Doberman can figure out how far from home your dog has wandered.

When vacationing with your dog, have a tag made that includes the phone number where you'll be staying and the number of a contact person who could be called in your

FAST FACT

The owners of some show and breeding dogs have DNA profiles created of their animals as a means of identification. However, this practice remains rare among pet owners.

absence. If there's no time to get a separate tag engraved with your vacation contact numbers, write them in waterproof pen on a piece of cloth adhesive tape, and stick this on top of his regular tag.

The drawback of tags is that they can be lost or deliberately removed, leaving no ID on your dog at all.

TATTOOS: This means of identification usually consists of a string of numbers and/or letters applied in permanent ink on the dog's inner thigh. The procedure takes only a few minutes and the sensation ranges from tickly to slightly painful, depending on the dog's sensitivity and the skill of the tattoo artist. The plus side of tattoo identification is its permanence: you can use the tattoo to prove that a "found" dog is yours. The downside is that, over time, the tattoo may become difficult to read, because the ink may fade or the characters may stretch as the dog grows.

For a fee, tattoo registries will keep a record of your dog's tattoo

When vacationing with your Doberman, pack a clearly focused photograph of him. That way, if he becomes lost, you'll have a picture available to make a lost dog poster.

number and your contact information. Many people finding a dog would not know to look for a tattoo, however, and even if they did find it, they couldn't contact you directly to reunite you with your dog.

MICROCHIPS: This newer form of permanent identification is becoming increasingly popular. A small computer chip, the size of a grain of wild rice, is implanted under the skin between the dog's shoulder blades. Each microchip is coded with a unique number, which is registered to the dog's owner through one of several microchip registries. If someone finds your lost Doberman, the staff at nearly any veterinary clinic or shelter in North America should be able to scan the dog's back with a special microchip reader. Your contact information will come up, and you will be contacted and reunited with your beloved pal. The one downside to this form of ID is that sometimes microchips will shift out of position, so the scanner can't read them properly.

SPAYING AND NEUTERING

Should you neuter your Doberman Pinscher? For several decades, neutering pets by removing their reproductive organs has been considered the politically correct thing to do.

According to the Humane Society of the United States, every year more than 3 million unwanted dogs are euthanized in animal shelters. The practice of spaying females or neutering males is intended to address this problem by preventing the birth of unwanted pups.

There are other good reasons to consider spaying or neutering your pet. Removing your Doberman's reproductive organs will eliminate some undesirable sexually driven behaviors. Intact male dogs are more likely to roam away from your property, especially if there's an intact female in the neighborhood. They also have a stronger tendency than their neutered counterparts to mark their territory with urine, or to develop aggressive behaviors such as "humping" the legs of visitors. Spaying a female Doberman suppresses her estrous cycle (commonly known as being "in heat"); with intact females, this can be accompanied by a messy discharge of blood. Spaying before the first heat cycle can also eliminate the risk of ovarian or uterine cancer, infections of the uterus, mammary tumors, and other diseases associated with the female's reproductive organs.

However, in recent years counterarguments have surfaced against neutering pets. Those who oppose spaying or neutering dogs point out that responsible owners can confine their dogs to prevent unwanted litters. They also note that, although some puppies are put to sleep, most animals euthanized at shelters are older dogs relinquished by their owners, not baby pups that couldn't find a home. In addition, some of the supposed health benefits of neutering have been called into question or proven to be false. For example, it was once believed that neutering would protect male dogs from prostate cancer, but recent studies have shown that castrated males actually have a higher risk of prostate cancer than intact males do. Nonetheless, neutered male dogs are much less likely to develop other common prostate problems as they age.

There are pros and cons to neutering, and dog owners need to educate themselves about both sides of this issue to make the best choice for their Doberman Pinscher. It may be a good idea to discuss this issue with a trusted veterinarian.

PET INSURANCE

A relatively recent development, pet insurance, will cover many of the bills if anything serious happens to your Doberman Pinscher, such as an accident or a major illness like cancer. If you have pet insurance, you won't have to make the difficult decision between treating your dog and

Pet insurance first became available more than 30 years ago. Hundreds of companies now provide insurance coverage for dogs, cats, and other pets.

putting him down because the treatment is too expensive. Several types of pet health insurance policies are available, and the right coverage could save you thousands of dollars in veterinary bills.

Veterinary health insurance for your Doberman can be a huge financial help if he encounters serious medical problems. However, the typical policy does not cover certain procedures and tests, so buyers should beware. For the most part, annual visits to the veterinary clinic, vaccinations, and elective procedures such as teeth cleaning or spaying/neutering are not covered by these insurance policies. Before purchasing a policy, read it carefully so you understand exactly what it covers and what's excluded.

CLEANING UP AFTER YOUR DOBERMAN PINSCHER

An obligation that, unfortunately, some dog owners ignore is cleaning up after their pets in public. This owner irresponsibility is one reason that certain parks and public areas are off-limits to dogs. Don't add to this problem—always carry a plastic bag or two when you walk your Doberman, and use it to pick up his poop so you can dispose of it in a garbage can. Keep a few bags handy in your car so that you're prepared when your Dobe accompanies you on trips.

Although cleaning up your Doberman's feces may not be pleasant, there are advantages to performing this chore. When picking up his waste, watch for stool that is off-color, contains blood or mucus, exhibits signs of parasites, or is particularly runny. These could be signs of a health problem.

OTHER LEGAL ISSUES

Just as you establish household rules so that you can live harmoniously with your dog in a human household, local and state governments establish laws so that your dog can live harmoniously in the community. Laws that pertain strictly to pet ownership are designed to promote safety for both humans and animals, and to address conflicts that often arise between the two species.

Make sure you know about any laws in your community relating to dog ownership. Some communities limit the number of dogs you may keep on your property. This helps to minimize nuisance complaints and guards against animal hoarding situations.

General nuisance laws in your community may or may not have a provision addressing dog ownership in particular, but dogs that bark incessantly—whether indoors or out—are considered a nuisance. Don't leave your dog unattended outside to bark and disturb your neighbors. If your dog is an inveterate barker, you must train him to eliminate this behavior.

Your community may also have a leash law that requires your dog to be on a leash any time he's off your property. This law is intended to encourage dog owners to keep their dogs under their control at all times. Dogs that are not under control can cause property damage, injuries, and even deaths. Under general liability laws, you are responsible for the actions of your Doberman, whether those actions occur on or off your premises. Any problems with aggression, in particular, should be addressed with the help of a professional trainer.

Thanks to strict state requirements requiring rabies vaccinations for all dogs, rabies transmission from dogs to humans in the United States is now almost nonexistent. Unfortunately, this lethal virus still permeates the wild animal population, so it's crucial to have your dog vaccinated against rabies. Make sure you know what the requirements are in your state. Most states require an

Obey local laws about cleaning up after your Doberman Pinscher.

initial vaccination plus a three-year booster, while others require an annual rabies booster.

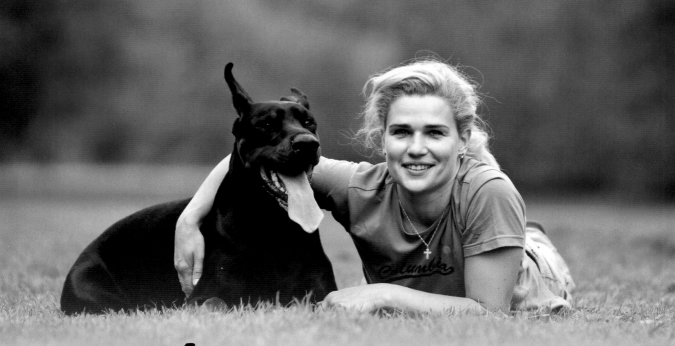

CHAPTER FOUR

Finding the Right Doberman

While all Doberman Pinschers share certain physical characteristics—or they would not be Doberman Pinschers—no two individual Dobermans are exactly alike. Some will be the kind of dog you are looking for, while others will have traits that don't appeal to you. Here are some tips to help you find a Doberman Pinscher that will be a good match for you and your family.

FACTORS TO CONSIDER

GENDER: One important decision you will need to make is whether you want a male or a female Doberman Pinscher. Some people believe that male Dobermans make better guards,

Before bringing a Doberman home, consider how he'll fit with your family and lifestyle.

or that females are more affectionate. However, these traits are not linked to gender. Both male and female Dobermans can be equally affectionate and equally protective.

Male Dobermans are usually taller and stronger than females, and a male's head is usually larger and broader. Some people are attracted to that larger, stronger, more masculine appearance, so they choose a male. On the other hand, some people prefer the slightly smaller size and more feminine look of the female Doberman.

Most Doberman Pinschers make friends more easily and get along better with friendly dogs of the opposite sex. This is particularly common with Dobermans that are intact (not spayed or neutered). If you already have a Doberman and want to add another to your household, consider the way your current dog behaves around others of the same sex. If your current pet does not get along with dogs of the same gender, save yourself some frustration by choosing a Doberman of the opposite sex. If your current dog gets along well with both sexes, he will probably accept a new housemate dog of either gender.

YOUR GOALS: Choosing the right Doberman Pinscher will be easier if you have some ideas about what you would like your dog to accomplish. Are you interested in competitive sports, like Obedience, Agility, Tracking, or Herding competitions? Would you like to exhibit your dog in Conformation shows? Would you like to get involved in pet-assisted therapy, which involves taking your trained Doberman Pinscher to visit

The temperamental and personality differences between male and female Doberman Pinschers are very modest. Male dogs are slightly larger and more muscular than females.

people in hospitals and nursing homes? To find a good candidate for any of these pursuits, seek out breeders whose Dobermans have excelled in the sports or activities that interest you most.

Good training and the right kind of stimulation can strengthen and enhance a dog's inherited potential, but for him to excel in a particular activity that potential must be present in the first place. You're more likely to find that potential in a pup whose parents and other relatives already demonstrate that ability. If you have a specific sport or activity in mind for a Doberman Pinscher you are considering, but are fairly new to that activity yourself, have someone with experience evaluate the pup or dog before you make your final decision

HOW TO FIND A RESPONSIBLE BREEDER

The Doberman Pinscher Club of America (DPCA) has a code of ethics that serves as a guideline for the ethical breeding and sale of Doberman Pinschers. Members of

Don't choose the first adorable Doberman puppy you see. Instead, watch the puppies and see how they interact with each other. For a beginning dog owner, the ideal puppy is one that is neither too bold nor too timid.

DPCA agree to maintain the highest standards of health, cleanliness, and care for the Doberman Pinschers they breed. This includes physical care, such as proper diet, exercise, and veterinary treatment, as well as psychological care, including training and proper socialization.

A puppy or dog from a breeder who adheres to the DPCA breeder's code should be clean, healthy, and confident. The code of ethics requires all Dobermans considered for breeding to be tested for hip dysplasia and other inherited health problems known to affect the breed. Breeders are expected to provide their customers with complete health records, a three-generation pedigree, and the proper paperwork to register the puppy they have purchased. The code also requires breeders to help with problems or provide information throughout the dog's life. You'll have a better chance of finding a responsible and reputable Doberman Pinscher breeder if you choose from among those who are members in good standing of DPCA and have signed on to the breeder's code.

Be selective when choosing a breeder. Even if you're not looking for a show-quality Doberman Pinscher, it's best to avoid "puppy mills"—kennels where large numbers of dogs are bred in unhealthy condi-

Look for a puppy that appears happy and healthy, with bright eyes and a clean coat.

tions. Many of the dogs that come from these types of places are not properly cared for or socialized.

Before you pick up your puppy, take a good look around the breeder's property. Is it clean? Do the dogs appear to be well fed and healthy? You should be able to answer yes to both of these questions. Don't think this assessment process is a one-way street, though. A serious breeder will want to know that her quality puppies will be going to good homes. She may ask you about other family members, their ages, and how they feel about dogs. She will ask whether you have a fenced-in backyard or someplace else nearby where your Doberman Pinscher can get the exercise he needs. And she will probably discuss proper nutrition and health care for your puppy.

ADOPTING FROM A SHELTER OR BREED RESCUE

Another option is adopting a dog from a shelter or rescue organization. Doberman Pinschers are given up for adoption for many reasons, and often they have nothing to do with any flaws in the dog himself. Most dogs are surrendered to shelters because of changes in the

BREED RESCUE ORGANIZATIONS

Breeders and others who love Doberman Pinschers volunteer their time, talents, and resources to help Dobermans (and sometimes Doberman mixes) that lose their homes. Nonprofit breed rescue groups exist for most breeds. Some are small, independent, local rescues, while others are larger and more organized, with national and regional groups connected closely through a network of volunteers. There are organizations in every state dedicated to rescuing Doberman Pinschers.

Rescuing Doberman Pinschers can be expensive, with the cost of veterinary care, food, transport, equipment, phone, mailing expenses, and hundreds of other miscellaneous needs. Funds are quickly used to help the dogs, so more money is always needed. Although animal-loving philanthropists will sometimes donate a large sum to a rescue organization, these groups must usually raise most of the money they need to operate. Rescue volunteers may hold bake sales, garage sales, auctions, dog-walkathons, and whatever other fundraisers they can think of to bring in needed donations.

Rescue groups always need more volunteers, and there are jobs for anyone willing to help. Rescue organizations need people to foster adoptable dogs, groom and exercise dogs, organize fundraisers, check out the homes of prospective adopters and make follow-up visits after adoptions, help with paperwork and office chores, or even make a couple dozen cupcakes for a bake sale. If you can lend a hand to your local or regional Doberman rescue group, it will be greatly appreciated. More important, it will help homeless Doberman Pinschers.

owner's situation. For example, the owner gets a job in a new town and cannot take her dog along, a child in the family develops an allergy to the dog, or the owner dies and no one in the family wants her dog.

Some dogs end up in shelters and rescue organizations because their previous owner could not manage their behavior or temperament. Most of these dogs are not rejects, however, just unfortunate victims of circumstance. You can find wonderful Doberman Pinschers in shelters and rescues, and one might be the perfect companion for you.

When you adopt a dog in this way, the workers at the shelter or rescue may not be able to provide much information about his past. Ask the volunteers who are handling the adoption process to tell you as much as they can about the dog's behavior while he was in the organization's care. If you're not very experienced with Dobermans, when you go to meet the dog you are thinking of adopting, take along someone who is familiar with the breed. If you don't have an experienced friend, consider hiring a dog trainer to evaluate the prospective adoptee. Make sure the trainer understands the qualities that are important to you, so she helps you pick the right dog.

No matter how much care you take before selecting a dog from a rescue or shelter, you could still be in for surprises after you've had your Doberman Pinscher for several months. Newly adopted dogs are often on their best behavior for about three months after the adoption. During that three-month period, the dog will settle in and get comfortable in his new home. Once he feels at home with you, he may start relaxing and behaving differently. Sometimes those "new" behaviors,

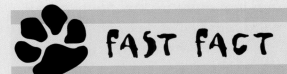

FAST FACT

If your adopted Doberman Pinscher is obviously purebred but you don't have his registration papers, he won't be eligible to compete in Conformation events. However, the lack of papers doesn't have to keep him out of other competitive events, such as Agility or Obedience trials. You can apply to the American Kennel Club for a Purebred Alternative Listing (PAL). To receive the PAL number, your Doberman Pinscher will have to be spayed or neutered. The AKC will issue your dog a number that will enable you to enter him in competitive events. You can download the application form from the AKC's Web site, or ask questions about the program by emailing PAL@akc.org.

FAST FACT

Observing pups at play with their litter-mates can give you a good idea of how curious and how bold they will be as adults.

which surface months after the adoption, are really old habits that got the dog into trouble with his last owner. As those behaviors appear, be prepared to manage the situation and the dog's environment while you teach him more acceptable behavior.

Puppies can sometimes be found in shelters or through rescue organizations. However, most of the dogs available from these sources will probably be adolescents or adults. If you're determined to start with a puppy, you may have to wait a while before one becomes available. There are some benefits to adopting adolescent or adult dogs, though. When you adopt an older Doberman, he may already be housetrained and know some obedience cues and other useful skills. You'll also have a better idea of his temperament.

WHAT TO LOOK FOR IN A PUPPY AND ITS PARENTS

Before you go looking at litters of pups, think about the temperament and personality you'd like in your dog. Puppies are so cute that it's easy to fall in love with them, but not every pup will be right for you. Handle and observe the pups for a while, then decide whether one is the right animal companion.

By the time a pup is seven weeks old, his natural personality and temperament will be fairly easy to recognize if you know what to look for. You can learn a lot about a puppy by observing him interacting with his siblings. Watch how littermates play, and note which pups act bossy and which get bossed around. Place a large object, like an open cardboard box, in the puppy play area and watch what they do with it. Some pups will explore it, others may ignore it, and some may wait and watch what the others do, then mimic their actions. This experiment will give you an idea of how each pup approaches unfamiliar situations.

FAST FACT

The best way to keep unwanted old habits from re-emerging in an adopted dog is enroll him in a training class right away. This will help your dog learn good habits for his new life with you.

PAPERS THE BREEDER PROVIDES

When you buy a purebred Doberman Pinscher, the breeder should provide all the paperwork necessary for pedigree registration when she sends the dog home with you. If you don't receive all the paperwork when you pick up your Doberman puppy, if may be more difficult to obtain it later.

When you purchase a puppy, the breeder should provide a signed copy of the application form she got from the AKC (or other registry) when she registered the litter. This will enable you to register the pup yourself. The breeder should also provide a three-generation pedigree, along with the dog's vaccination and health certification records. If the puppy has received a permanent ID, such as a microchip or tattoo, the breeder will supply this information as well.

If the dog is an adult, the breeder simply has to sign his registration over to you as the new owner.

Pups tend to keep the same personality and temperament traits as they mature, so imagine those traits in a grown dog. That may help you decide which pup would fit best your needs and goals.

If the parents of the pups or any adult relatives are available, take a look at them, too. Puppies grow up resembling their relatives, so physical and temperamental traits of the adults are likely to appear in the puppy when he matures. If you have aspirations for competition, seek a litter with parents who are accomplished in the events that interest you. Parent dogs with talent and drive are likely to produce offspring with potential for the same winning characteristics.

Dogs that are curious, bold, and very persistent tend to do well in competitive sports like Agility, Obedience, and Conformation. Pups with these characteristics are usually very "busy," both physically and mentally, and they typically require more training and attention to keep them out of mischief. Not everyone wants or needs a dog like that. People who want dogs mainly as companions usually prefer less intense dogs than people who train their dogs for competition in performance events.

CHAPTER Five

Caring for Your Puppy (Birth to Six Months)

To prepare for your new puppy, you'll need to get your home and family ready for the new arrival. Establish the rules before you bring the pup home and make sure all household members, including children, understand the rules and reasons behind them. People tend to follow rules better if they have helped to develop them, so ask family members for input while you're planning for your puppy's arrival.

Puppies explore their surroundings by playing with and chewing whatever draws their attention. This curiosity can be destructive or even dangerous if your home has not been puppy-proofed. This must be done

It will take time for a new dog to make the transition into your home.

FAST FACT

Children tend to follow rules better when allowed to help make them. Include your children in the rule-making process about what your new puppy will be allowed to do and how the puppy should be treated.

before your puppy comes into your home for the first time.

A pup's view of the world is different from yours—he sees everything from closer to the floor. Things look different from that perspective, so get down to puppy level and take a look around. Anything that sticks out or hangs down will immediately attract a pup's attention, which means he'll probably tug on or chew it. Remove those items or block your pup's access to them. Don't just make it challenging for your new Doberman to reach those things. Your puppy may be up to the challenge, so make it impossible.

SUPPLIES YOU'LL NEED

Before you bring a Doberman Pinscher puppy home, you'll want to acquire certain essential supplies. One item is a dog crate. The crate has many uses. A crate becomes your dog's "den," his place to go when he wants to relax. Many dogs choose to sleep in their crates at night. You'll find the crate helpful when house-training your Doberman, because a dog—even a puppy—will try not to poop or pee in the place where he sleeps. The crate will also come in handy when doors are being opened or a lot of people are in the house, and your dog can stay inside his crate when you're away from the house.

Dog crates are usually made of hard plastic or wire mesh. The crate should be large enough that your dog can stand up, turn around, and lie down in it without being too restricted. If the crate is too large, however, your puppy may go to the bathroom in a corner, defeating its purpose as

A wire crate provides a safe place where your Doberman Pinscher can sleep or escape from household activity.

Your Doberman Pinscher will need a collar that fits comfortably around his neck and carries his identification tag and any others required, such as proof of licensing or rabies vaccination. The Dobe pictured above is also wearing a harness that attaches to a leash. This type of arrangement puts less strain on a dog's neck and windpipe when he's walking.

a housetraining tool. You may have to buy two crates: one to fit your puppy, and a larger one when he's full grown. There are also adjustable crates available; these contain a divider that can be moved to enlarge the den area as your dog grows. Your Doberman will be comfortable if you put some old towels, a blanket, or a

small piece of rug into the bottom of his crate.

Another item that will come in quite handy is a baby gate or two. These accordion-like wood or plastic barriers can be used to keep your puppy confined in certain spaces with easy-to-clean tile floors, such as the kitchen or laundry room. This is best when you're going to be away from home for more than three hours, as a puppy should not be locked up in a crate for too long.

There are many types and styles of collars, so pick one that appeals to you. As your dog is growing, make sure to check his collar regularly to make sure it does not get too tight. You should be able to easily slip two fingers between your dog's neck and the collar. If it's tight, loosen the collar or move up to a larger collar size. Your dog will probably reach his final collar size by the time he's two years old.

You may also want to purchase a training collar. These usually consist of a chain that tightens around the dog's neck when pulled. Remember, never leave the training collar on your dog when you're not around, as this type of collar can become caught on furniture or shrubbery and strangle your dog.

The standard dog leash is six feet (1.8 meters), long and it has a metal clasp on one end so you can attach it to your pet's training collar. At the other end is a loop through which you can slip your hand to keep a tight grip. Often, the owners of larger dogs like Dobermans will wrap the leash once around their hand for an even more secure grip. This can be helpful in case your Doberman suddenly lunges at another dog. If you do this, a leather or cotton web leash may be more comfortable than a nylon leash.

When looking for food and water bowls, stainless steel or ceramic dishes work best. They are harder for your dog to overturn, and they're more durable. Plastic bowls may get chewed, and they're more likely to retain bacteria.

Last—but certainly not least in your dog's mind—you'll need toys to entertain your Doberman. Your new pal will need hard, durable chewing toys to work his jaws and teeth, squeaky toys for good old-fashioned fun, balls and disks like Frisbees to chase outdoors, and soft stuffed toys that he'll enjoy carrying when she's feeling mellow.

Remember, you'll want to take the crate, collar, and leash with you when you pick up your puppy, so that you can safely transport him to his new home.

WHAT TO EXPECT WHEN YOUR PUP FIRST COMES HOME

Usually, during the first night home with a new pup, no one gets a full night's sleep. The puppy is used to sleeping with his littermates, so the first night without them he may whine or howl a

(Above) Cotton mesh leashes will feel more comfortable in your hand than a leash made from nylon. (Right) Stainless steel food and water bowls resist chewing and are diffi-cult for your Doberman to knock over.

sad lament for a while after you put him to bed.

To ease your new puppy's loneliness, let him sleep in a crate or a pen in your bedroom. Your pup will be comforted by being able to see, hear, and smell your presence, and won't feel so lonely in the unfamiliar new surroundings. It may also help to play soft music in the background when you put your puppy to bed. Soothing music will calm him, so eventually you'll both be able to sleep. If the breeder gave you an old blanket or toy when you picked up your Doberman puppy, put that in the crate. The familiar scent will be comforting.

Here's another suggestion: play with your new pup for an hour or so before bedtime. That way, he'll be tired and will more likely fall asleep of his own accord.

Remember, it's not a good idea to leave a young pup in a crate for more than a few hours at a time. You'll need to wake a few times during the night to let him out of his crate to eliminate.

PUPPY NUTRITION

A Doberman Pinscher puppy needs a balanced diet. His food should be easy to digest, rich in high-quality proteins and fats, and contain all the vitamins and minerals needed to

Where you feed your Doberman Pinscher is up to you, but a quiet spot where he can enjoy his food uninterrupted and not make a mess will work best for everyone. A quiet corner in the kitchen is ideal.

nourish his rapidly growing body. In the puppy's first few weeks, his mother's milk meets all these requirements. The mother dog's milk contains colostrum, which transfers to the puppies the mother's immunity to diseases for which she has been vaccinated. This maternal immunity lasts until the pups are between two and four months old, protecting the litter from dangerous viruses until they are old enough to receive vaccinations of their own.

As each pup is born, the dam, or mother dog, licks her pup to clean and stimulate him, then guides the pup to a teat to start nursing. The dam nurses her puppies for several weeks, even though the needle-sharp baby teeth will cause her pain.

When puppies are around five or six weeks old, their mother will have trouble keeping up with their appetites. At this time the breeder will begin to wean them onto soft solid foods, like baby cereal or ground meat thinned to a gruel with water or mother's milk. When puppies first start lapping up this food, they usually end up wearing as much of it as they swallow. By the time you pick up your puppy, he should be fully weaned to solid food.

Doberman Pinscher puppies need a lot of nutrients, particularly protein and fat, to support healthy growth and provide energy. The younger your pup, the more often he will need to eat each day. It is best to feed your pup meals spaced apart fairly evenly at about the same times each day.

From weaning to about ten weeks of age, a puppy will need at least four meals a day. From ten weeks to about four months, a pup will need to eat three times a day, plus maybe a light snack before bedtime. When the pup is four or five months old, you can eliminate one of the meals. The two-meal-a-day schedule can be maintained for the rest of the dog's life.

Adult dogs can remain healthy eating just one daily meal. However, most dogs are more comfortable being fed twice a day. Dividing your Doberman's daily ration into two smaller meals will help keep him from feeling overly hungry for long periods. Also, two smaller meals put less stress on the dog's digestive system. This is a sensible way to feed a Doberman Pinscher, as it helps reduce the chance for bloat, a painful and potentially dangerous disorder that is fairly common in this breed (see pages 60–62).

There is no one "best" diet for Doberman Pinschers. People have strong preferences when it comes to dog food, but dogs can do well on a number of different diets. Between you and your veterinarian, you should determine a diet that your dog will thrive on, and that's what you should feed him.

COGNITIVE DEVELOPMENT AND SOCIALIZATION

As the days and weeks go by, your Doberman pup's brain will be growing and maturing. Your pup will begin to understand better how the world works. His attention span will grow longer, he'll figure things out more quickly, and he'll be able to learn more new skills and do more with what he knows.

Socialization is one of the most important things you can do to help your Doberman Pinscher develop into a well-adjusted, self-assured adult dog. The more people, animals, and new situations a puppy encounters, the more confident and accepting he will be as an adult. The reason for socialization training is to help the pup discover that the world is a friendly place, for the most part, and that the people, animals, and situations he will encounter are interesting but generally harmless.

Try to introduce your puppy to between three and five new people a week. The people should represent as many variations of the human form as possible. Let your pup meet tall, short, old, and young people. Introduce him to men with facial hair; women with big hats; kids on skates, scooters, and boards; runners and hikers; bicyclists and people with motorcycles; folks of all sizes, shapes, and colors. Make sure the people he meets are friendly and gentle, and don't let them do anything that frightens him.

Socialization also includes letting your pup meet friendly dogs and cats and observe large animals like hors-

Playing with your Doberman puppy allows him to get the exercise he needs for good health while also exposing him to new people, animals, and situations.

es, cows, or llamas. When socializing your pup around large animals be sure to keep him on a leash so he doesn't get hurt. When choosing dogs and cats to introduce your pup to, determine first if they're friendly to pups. If you introduce your Doberman to a "friendly" animal that tries to intimidate or hurt your puppy, he will lose faith in your ability to determine safe from unsafe.

Be careful not to overwhelm your pup. Figure out how much he can handle, and avoid pushing him past that point. Overwhelming your Doberman with too much at once may create fear or anxiety instead of dispelling these emotions.

A Puppy Kindergarten class is a great place for your Doberman pup to meet and play with other dogs his age. You and the class instructor will both be there to make sure the play goes well and no pups bully others. Playtime and lesson time alternate in a good Puppy Kindergarten class, so your pup learns to come and pay attention to you, even with several puppy pals nearby.

For animals other than dogs, it is often safest to let the pup see, hear, and smell them but not allow physical contact, particularly if the animals are not yours and you do not know whether they are gentle with pups. Go near enough to them that your pup can satisfy his curiosity but stay far enough away that everyone remains safe.

Some people avoid taking their pups out to socialize and meet the world until they have received all their immunizations. Unfortunately, by that time the main window of opportunity for socializing a pup has usually passed, and the pup may have developed a fear of the unfamiliar. It is a longer and more complicated process to socialize a puppy that has been isolated most of his first six months.

GROOMING AND BATHING

With their short, smooth coat, Doberman Pinschers are an easy breed to groom. A brisk daily brushing with a soft-bristled brush will remove dust and loose hair and an occasional bath with mild shampoo will keep your Doberman shiny, clean, and odor-free.

Dogs don't sweat the way humans do, so they don't need to bathe as frequently. However, the natural oils in a Doberman Pinscher's coat can sometimes give the coat a slight odor. Coat oils also pick up and hold dirt and grime from the environment. Your Doberman will feel better when he's clean after a bath, and it's more pleasant to pet and cuddle a nice-smelling dog whose coat is clean and

A brush with soft bristles, or a pet grooming glove, can be used to keep your Doberman's coat in top condition.

shiny. One bath a month should be enough, as bathing too much can make your Doberman's skin dry.

Some dogs dislike baths, but you can make bathing more pleasant for your dog if you go about it the right way. Here are some tips to help you make bathing easier for both you and your dog:

- Prepare the tub by placing a nonskid rubber tub mat on the bottom, so your dog will have good traction and not hurt himself by slipping and sliding.
- Keep the drain open and do not fill the tub. Dogs usually prefer this to standing in slippery, soapy water.
- Take a couple dozen small yummy treats into the bathing area with you, and dole them out to your Doberman every few minutes during his bath.

- Wet down your dog's coat with lukewarm water (cooler than people usually like for bathing, about 70°F/21°C), using the shower wand or a plastic pitcher. Try not to get your Doberman's head wet yet. Once a dog's head gets wet, he will want to shake off the water. Waiting until the end to wash his head and face will keep you drier during the bathing process.
- Put about a quarter cup (60 ml) of shampoo in a gallon (4 liter) jug and fill the jug with lukewarm water. This diluted shampoo will be much easier to work into your Doberman's coat, and it will take less time and water to rinse it out of the coat.
- Apply shampoo and lather it through the coat, starting at the neck and working toward the tail.
- Keep your dog's head and face dry until the end of the bath.

Any time water accidentally splashes on his face, quickly wipe it off with a dry towel.

- Rinse your dog, starting with the head and working back toward his tail. Rinse him until the water running down the drain is clear and has no more bubbles. Then rinse him one more time. If any shampoo is left in the coat, it will attract dirt. This will make your dog's coat sticky and stinky, and he'll need another bath too soon.
- Dry your Doberman as thoroughly as possible with towels. If the weather is cool, keep him inside until he is completely dry, to avoid a chill.

NAIL CARE

Your Doberman Pinscher's nails need to be trimmed regularly or they will grow excessively long and sharp. Long toenails can deliver nasty scratches. They can also start curling inward as they grow, increasing the risk that the nail will snag on something and be torn off. A torn-off nail is quite painful, so avoid that by trimming your Doberman's nails frequently.

Nail trimming should be done every week. However, a trim every two weeks can still keep a Doberman's nails in good shape. If you let it go longer than that, the blood vessels and nerves in the living tissue inside the nail (called the "quick") will grow too close to the end of the nail. This will make it difficult to trim your dog's nails without nicking the quick and causing your dog pain.

You can trim your dog's nails with special scissors or clippers made for pet nails. If you do not feel confident using tools with blades on your dog's nails, you could instead file them down using a convex file specially designed for dogs' nails. If that is too

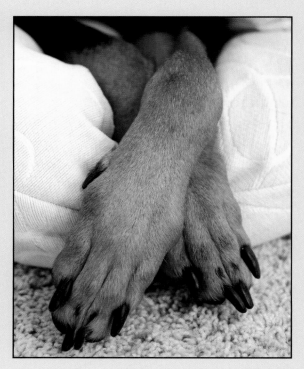

Your Doberman's nails don't have to be trimmed back too far. Just clip off the tip of each nail, so that you don't accidentally hit the quick and cause bleeding and pain.

slow, try shortening your Doberman's nails with an electric rotary tool, similar to those used in nail salons.

To trim the nails, support the dog's paw and steady the toe you are working on. Trim off just the tip of the nail. Don't cut off too much, or you'll hurt the dog. If you cut too deep, you will nick the blood vessels that feed the nail, causing bleeding and pain. Commercial blood coagulant powders are available at pet supply stores. These powders will quickly stop a nail from bleeding when it's cut too short. Buy some and keep it on hand, just in case.

DENTAL CARE

Clean teeth and healthy gums are important to your Doberman's overall health. Food residue that remains on teeth after eating promotes the growth of bacteria and formation of plaque. This will make the dog's breath smell bad, but that is the least of the concerns. Hardened plaque on a dog's teeth can irritate the gums, leading to infections. Bacteria from gum infections can find their way into the bloodstream and travel to the heart. If that bacteria infects the dog's heart valves, serious illness or death may result.

Dogs can keep their teeth fairly clean by chewing on kibble, bones,

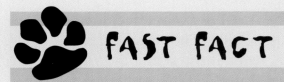

FAST FACT

Show grooming for a Doberman Pinscher is really no different from ordinary day-to-day grooming. Some breeds take all day to prepare for the ring, but a bath, a brushing, and a nail trim are all a Doberman Pinscher needs to look splendid in the show ring.

or chew toys, but often that's not enough for optimal dental health. You'll need to brush your Doberman Pinscher's teeth daily to prevent plaque buildup. Use a toothpaste specially formulated for dogs, as human toothpastes contain chemicals that can be harmful to your pet, and they won't like the minty flavor anyway. You can either use a regular toothbrush or a finger brush to clean your Doberman's teeth.

Once plaque has hardened, you may not be able to remove it by brushing. When this happens, the dog should have his teeth cleaned by your veterinarian. Many dogs need a professional dental cleaning annually, and some require cleaning twice a year. Keep an eye on your dog's mouth. If you see a hard whitish, brownish, or yellowish buildup on your dog's teeth at the gum line, schedule a professional cleaning.

HOUSETRAINING YOUR DOBERMAN PINSCHER

All dogs need to learn the manners required for living with humans. Teaching clean elimination habits is one of the first training challenges you'll face with your pup. You can make housetraining easier by establishing a consistent routine. Put your pup on a regular eating schedule and he will have more predictable elimination times. Give him frequent opportunities to use the designated potty area, and that will help prevent messy accidents in the house.

Teach your Doberman a cue word or phrase for elimination. Pick something you won't be embarrassed to say when you're out in public. Popular cues include "Go potty," "Do business," or "Hurry up." Say the cue when your pup is in the area you want him to use. Wait patiently until he goes, then quietly and calmly praise him.

When your pup has potty accidents—and all pups do—don't scold or punish him. Scolding can make your pup avoid you when he has to eliminate. Instead, he may start going behind furniture or in an unused room, where you won't notice that he's gone potty until your nose tells you there's a problem.

FAST FACT

Do not use ammonia-based products to clean housetraining accidents. Ammonia is similar to the scent of urine and may encourage the dog to soil that spot again.

If you see your pup start to eliminate indoors, call his name, clap your hands, or say something to get his attention. Then tell him, "Outside! Potty outside!" and quickly escort him to the approved area. At the potty place, calmly encourage him to eliminate, and then praise him when he does. Don't punish him for eliminating in an improper place.

If you don't catch your pup in time and you discover a potty accident, get a paper towel and take the pup back to the accident. Don't scold or shame him, just calmly blot up the pee or pick up the poop in the paper towel, then gently escort your pup to the elimination area. Smear the pee or drop the poop there, then step back and calmly praise your pup, "Good potty outside," as you would if he had gone there to begin with. Your puppy will learn that there's a "good place" to do potty business, and with your help and patience he will learn to use that area.

THE POTTY BELL

One very common cause of housetraining accidents is a puppy's inability to let someone know when he needs to go outside. You can resolve this issue easily by teaching your pup to ring a bell when he needs to go outside for a potty break.

Hang a bell on a cord and tie it around the handle of the door closest to your pup's outdoor potty area. You won't have to teach your pup to ring it, just ring it yourself before opening the door each time you take him out to eliminate.

Your pup will soon notice the connection between the bell ringing and the door opening, and will wonder if the bell causes the door to open. Within about a week after you start ringing the bell, he will give it a try himself. When he does, praise him and open the door for him. Once your Doberman realizes that he can "make" you open the door for him by ringing that bell, he will use the bell to signal you whenever he needs to go out.

ESTABLISHING HOUSEHOLD RULES

The best time to establish household rules is when you first get your pup. The rules are up to you, but generally they will include not begging for food at the dining table, not jumping on family members or guests to greet them, not barking incessantly, and not jumping on the furniture.

Don't allow your puppy to do things you would not find acceptable in an adult Doberman. If, for example, you allow your pup on furniture, he will want to lounge there as an adult. If you are sure that will be okay with you, go ahead and invite him onto the couch. However, if you don't want an adult Doberman on your sofa or bed, set that rule while your pup is young and stick to it.

If you start with one set of rules, then try to change them when your dog gets older, he'll become confused. It's much harder to change an established habit than install a good one, so think about how you'll want your Doberman Pinscher to behave as an adult, and help him learn those behaviors while he's young and impressionable.

Consistency is one of the hallmarks of good training technique. Make sure you give your Doberman consistent guidelines to follow, and enforce the rules you set up fairly.

CHAPTER SIX

Your Doberman's Health

Once a puppy enters your care, it will be up to you to keep him healthy. Maintaining a dog's good health takes work, but it's easier and less expensive than treating a serious disease or injury. Make sure your puppy gets everything he needs for good heath, including clean water, nourishing food, daily exercise, appropriate immunizations, and regular veterinary exams.

CHOOSING A VETERINARIAN

Next to you, the veterinarian is your dog's most important ally in maintaining good health over his lifetime. If you don't already have a veterinarian for your pup, you need to find

Finding a veterinarian that you trust is one of the most important things you can do to help ensure that your Doberman Pinscher lives a long and healthy life.

one and schedule a wellness exam. Don't wait until your dog really needs a veterinarian; instead, arrange for him to meet the veterinarian during a period of normal health. Doberman Pinschers can sometimes be wary of strangers, so meeting the veterinarian under pleasant conditions will help your Doberman accept being handled by the doctor or members of her staff during future visits.

To find a good veterinarian for your Doberman Pinscher, start by asking your dog-owning friends and acquaintances, especially those with medium or large dogs, which veterinarians they use. If several friends like and recommend the same veterinarian, that would be a good sign.

Another sign to look for is the one in the veterinarian's office that says AAHA. That stands for American Animal Hospital Association, an educational organization that helps those in veterinary practice to maintain the highest standards of animal care. The American Animal Hospital Association accredits only those veterinarians and clinics that meet its standards.

Consider also the distance from your home to the veterinary clinic. If your Doberman becomes sick or injured, a long trip to the clinic can waste precious time better spent

Ideally, a prospective veterinary clinic should be a member of the American Animal Hospital Association or a similar organization that inspects and accredits veterinary facilities.

with the doctor. So if you have a choice between two equally good veterinarians, but one's office is within a fifteen-minute drive while the other is an hour away, it makes more sense to choose the doctor that is closer.

Take into consideration whether your veterinary clinic is open twenty-four hours a day. If not, you'll need to make arrangements in case a medical emergency occurs during off-hours. Find out what your veterinarian's policies are for handling off-hours emergencies. Some rural veterinarians will rush from home at any hour and open the clinic for a patient with a true emergency, but that kind of service is rare and vanishing fast.

In some places, local veterinarians form an alliance or co-op to handle off-hours emergencies, each taking a turn on call overnight and on weekends and holidays. Many urban and suburban areas have emergency veterinary clinics that stay open 24/7, or clinics that are only open during off-hours.

Once you have lined up one or more veterinarians who sound good, plan a visit to the animal hospital for an interview and a hospital tour. Make an appointment for this and expect to pay for the vet's time. Veterinarians are usually very busy, and any time they spend answering your questions is time they would otherwise spend with their animal patients.

Look for a veterinary clinic that is located close to your home. If your Doberman Pinscher has a medical emergency, you'll want to get to the clinic within 20 to 30 minutes.

THE FIRST VISIT TO THE VETERINARY CLINIC

Although some veterinary clinics do accept walk-in clients, most will require an appointment to see the doctor. When you get to the veterinary clinic, leave your dog in the car, if possible, while you check in at the front desk. There will be paperwork to fill out for the new patient's file, and that will be easier without an excited or worried pup on your hands.

Bring along the health records the breeder gave you as well as any medical information you have on your puppy's parents. The vet will be asking questions about your pup's medical history, and that information may be important.

When you check in, ask if the vet's appointments are running on schedule. Sometimes your veterinarian may get tied up with an emergency, so caring for that animal becomes the top priority. That emergency case will take time that wasn't scheduled and the day's appointments may start running late.

If you arrive early or find that an unscheduled emergency is causing a delay of more than fifteen minutes, keep your dog outside. He will probably stay calmer and be more comfortable if you sit in the car with him or take him for a walk instead of the two of you hanging around the waiting room. He'll also be less likely to contract illnesses from animals with contagious diseases in the waiting room. Be back in the clinic at least five minutes before your pup's turn with the veterinarian. Any time you leave the waiting area, tell the staff where you'll be, in case the doctor is ready sooner than expected.

WHAT TO EXPECT AT A VETERINARY EXAM

When the veterinarian examines your pup, she will run her hands all over him. She will palpate his abdomen, checking for hernias, muscle tone, and any lumps or irregularities. She will feel his legs, hips, elbows, and check them for signs of dysplasia, a hereditary malformation of the hip socket or the top of the thigh bone. While doing this, she'll be alert for signs of tenderness or stiffness in your puppy's joints. The vet will

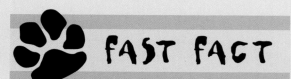

FAST FACT

Like puppies of other breeds, Doberman Pinscher puppies can carry parasitic worms that can infect other pets, as well as people. Your puppy must be tested—and, if necessary, treated—for worms as soon as possible.

check your puppy's skin for lumps, bumps, flea dirt, or anything else that doesn't belong there. She will listen to his heart for murmurs and check the sound of his lungs. She will examine his ears and eyes and check hearing and vision. She will look in his mouth and throat, and examine his teeth.

While the veterinarian examines your pup's body, she will also be observing his personality and degree of socialization. If she thinks your puppy needs more socialization or practice with body handling, she may suggest ways to do that or refer you to a trainer or behavior specialist who can teach you what to do and help you do it.

If your puppy has not been wormed or if he shows any signs of parasites, such as frequent unformed feces or a habit of rubbing his butt on the floor, take a fresh fecal sample to the veterinarian so it can be checked under a microscope. Only a small amount of feces is needed; a sample the size of a thimble should be plenty.

VACCINATIONS

Recent scientific studies are changing the way dogs are immunized against diseases. The long-accepted practice involved repeated shots at approximately two- to three-week intervals until a puppy was four months old, then providing annual immunization booster shots each year. That protocol is currently changing. Major veterinary schools have adopted new protocols that involve fewer

Following your vet's vaccination schedule will protect your pet pal from some very nasty diseases.

vaccinations and less-frequent boosters. Also, more veterinarians are tailoring their immunization recommendations to the individual needs of each dog, instead of vaccinating every dog in the same way.

At this point in time, some veterinarians still follow the old vaccination protocol, while others have switched to the new one. The best policy for dog owners is to follow the guidance of the veterinarian who knows your dog best. Once your Doberman has a clean bill of health, the veterinarian will administer any vaccinations that your pet is scheduled to receive at this stage of his development, according to the vaccination protocol the vet prefers.

The American Animal Hospital Association classifies vaccinations as core (recommended), non-core (optional), or not recommended. The "core" diseases that your Doberman Pinscher should be vaccinated against included the following:

CANINE ADENOVIRUS-2: Canine adenovirus-2 is an upper respiratory infection that causes a hacking cough. Although this virus is considered mild, the vaccine for this disease provides protection against a much more serious virus called canine adenovirus-1, also known as "infectious canine hepatitis." Canine adenovirus-1 causes the more serious consequences of jaundice and liver damage.

DISTEMPER: Distemper affects the nervous system and is fatal to 75 percent of infected puppies. Symptoms include eye and nasal discharge, severe listlessness, fever, vomiting and diarrhea.

PARVOVIRUS: Parvovirus is a highly contagious, gastrointestinal virus that causes high fevers, vomiting, and bloody diarrhea, and can also be fatal for puppies.

RABIES: By far, the most frightening and deadly of all dog diseases is rabies. This virus attacks the nervous system and causes symptoms ranging from throat paralysis and the inability to swallow (which causes the drooling commonly described as "frothing at the mouth") to delirium and extreme aggressiveness. Due to the seriousness of this disease, and its risk of transmission to humans, state laws require all dogs to be vaccinated against this disease.

According to the AAHA protocol, vaccinations against the following diseases are optional:

BORDETELLA: Also known as "kennel cough," bordetella is a common, highly contagious bacterial infection of the respiratory system that causes chronic coughing. This disease is not considered serious, but it's a good idea to vaccinate dogs that will come into regular contact with other dogs in a group setting, such as a kennel or dog show. The vaccine is administered through an intranasal spray.

LEPTOSPIROSIS: Leptospirosis is a bacterial disease that can damage the liver and kidneys. Symptoms range from fever and jaundice to the excessive consumption of water. Because leptospirosis is caused by bacteria, it can be treated with antibiotics.

LYME DISEASE: Lyme disease can cause fever, loss of appetite, arthritis, listlessness, and joint swelling. This vaccine is only recommended for dogs that live in areas where deer ticks, which carry the disease, are prevalent.

PARAINFLUENZA: Parainfluenza is a respiratory virus that is generally not serious itself, but can reduce your puppy's immunity to secondary infec-

Rabies is spread to dogs when they are bitten by infected wild animals, such as raccoons and bats.

tions like pneumonia. Symptoms include coughing and nasal discharge.

BREED-SPECIFIC HEALTH PROBLEMS

There are some health problems that tend to occur more commonly in certain dog breeds. Some of these conditions are hereditary, while others are just related to the breed's physical characteristics. Some common health issues among Doberman Pinschers include the following:

EXOCRINE PANCREATIC INSUFFICIENCY (EPI): This is a genetic condition found in Doberman Pinschers that causes a gradual deterioration of the part of the pancreas involved in protein digestion. When this occurs, the Doberman will lose weight and muscle steadily, even though he may be eating large amounts of food.

In addition to weight loss, a sign of EPI may include the passage of large amounts of soft, unformed feces. Some dogs with this disorder will eat their own feces as well as other non-food items. Other dogs with EPI may have bouts of intermittent vomiting and watery diarrhea.

EPI is hereditary and there is no cure, but in most cases it can be managed by giving the dog powdered pancreatic enzymes at mealtime. The enzyme supplement helps with the digestive process, so the dog can regain lost weight and his elimination becomes normal.

HIP DYSPLASIA: This condition is found in many medium and large breeds, including the Doberman Pinscher. Hip dysplasia is a malformation of the hip socket and/or the head of the femur (thigh bone). This abnormality can be painful or just uncomfortable, depending on how much the bone is deformed and if bone rubs against bone when the dog

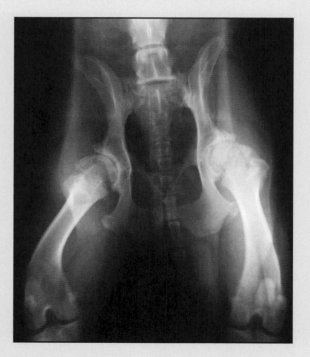

This X-ray of a Doberman Pinscher's hips shows the malformation of the femur and hip socket known as hip dysplasia.

moves. In serious cases, this disorder can make a dog lame.

Dysplasia has a hereditary component, but it is also affected by the care a dog receives. Overfeeding and excessive exercise can make dysplasia worse. It is best to keep pups on the lean side and be sensible about exercise.

According to the Orthopedic Foundation for Animals (OFA), about 6 percent of Dobermans develop hip dysplasia. Today, most responsible breeders will have the hips of prospective parent dogs examined in advance. X-rays are sent to the OFA, to determine whether the dogs are sound enough to breed. As this practice has grown more common, the incidence of hip dysplasia in the Doberman Pinscher has been reduced. However, because of the complex genes for dysplasia, it is unlikely that this disorder will ever be completely eradicated.

PANOSTEITIS: This is a condition related to the growth of the leg bones that can cause sudden lameness. The dogs most often affected are large and giant breeds under two years old. Panosteitis can appear in dogs as early as two months of age. The lameness usually starts in one or both front legs, then moves to the back legs. Sometimes the lameness will last a month or two, then disappear, only to suddenly return days or weeks later. Most dogs with panosteitis can recover with proper treatment.

VON WILLEBRAND'S DISEASE (vWD): This hereditary disorder is caused by a deficiency of a plasma protein necessary for proper clotting of the blood. It occurs in many breeds, but the breed with the highest incidence of this disorder is the Doberman Pinscher. Even a fairly mild cut or injury can put a Doberman with vWD at risk of fatal blood loss. There is no cure for this severe bleeding disorder, but there is a genetic test to determine whether a dog carries the gene for vWD. Dogs testing positive for the vWD gene should not be bred, as they can pass the disorder to their offspring.

WOBBLER'S SYNDROME (CERVICAL SPONDYLOPATHY): This neurological disorder compresses the spinal cord in the neck vertebrae. This compression affects the nerves, causing the dog to exhibit a wobbly, staggering gait. Wobbler's Syndrome appears with relative frequency in the Doberman Pinscher, causing pain, lameness, and atrophy of the shoulder muscles. This condition usually appears when dogs are over two years old.

The exact cause of Wobbler's Syndrome is not yet known, but there is most likely a genetic predisposition. Other contributing factors may include degenerative disk disease, excessive protein and/or calcium in the diet, and hyperextension injury to the neck. There is no cure for Wobbler's Syndrome, but supportive treatment and surgery to stabilize the vertebrae can make an afflicted Doberman more comfortable.

BLOAT AND TORSION

As a breed, Doberman Pinschers have a higher-than-average risk of experiencing a dangerous condition known as bloat. Bloat involves the sudden, rapid buildup of gas and foamy mucus within the stomach. The pressure of the gas causes the stomach to expand inside the abdominal cavity. The bloated stomach presses against the heart, lungs, and abdominal blood vessels. This restricts their function and creates a painful and terrifying situation for the dog.

Symptoms of bloat include unsuccessful attempts to vomit, increased anxiety and restlessness, and a swollen abdomen that may feel tight like a drum. Your Doberman will probably not act like himself, and may curl into a ball and whine or lick his stomach because he is uncomfortable.

Bloat can quickly become a life-threatening emergency, particularly if it is accompanied by torsion. This occurs when the stomach twists or rotates, pinching off its entrance from the esophagus and its exit through the duodenum. This traps water, food, gas, and foam inside, causing the stomach to swell even more. As a consequence, carbon dioxide builds up within the dog's blood because the abdominal pressure prevents the heart and lungs from cleansing and oxygenating the blood. The blood pressure drops, the body becomes toxic, and the stomach continues to painfully distend.

Bloat is an emergency that requires veterinary intervention. The effects of bloat and torsion can kill a dog in under an hour. If you think your dog is having an episode of bloat, take him to the veterinary hospital right away. Call to let the

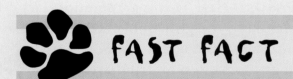

FAST FACT

The technical name for bloat with torsion is "Gastric Dilatation-Volvulus" (GDV). This condition occurs most frequently in deep-chested dogs over 40 pounds (18 kg).

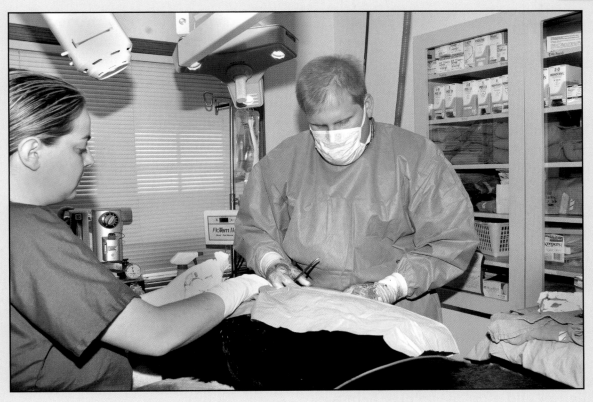

Bloat with torsion is an extremely dangerous condition, and emergency surgery may be required to save your Doberman Pinscher's life.

veterinarian know you are on the way with a dog suffering from bloat, then get there as quickly as you can.

When a dog comes in with bloat, the veterinarian will attempt to relieve the pressure by passing a large tube into the stomach by way of the mouth. If there is torsion, the tube will not get past that blockage. In this case, the only way to save the dog is to make an incision through the abdomen and into the stomach, so the gas can escape.

Once the pressure is relieved, the veterinarian can reposition the stomach. Dogs that experience bloating once will usually bloat again. To prevent torsion in future, the veterinarian will suture the stomach to the ribs so it cannot twist out of position if the dog bloats again.

The causes of bloat are not known for certain, though there seems to be a hereditary predisposition as well as a number of possible environmental and situational

FAST FACT

For several decades it was widely believed that elevating food and water bowls to the dog's chest height would help prevent bloat. However, a study by veterinarians at Purdue University showed that elevating the food bowl nearly doubles the likelihood for bloat.

triggers. Gulping air when eating may be one cause, so slowing down a fast eater can help. So can feeding two smaller meals per day instead of one big meal. Stress may be a contributing factor, so keeping your Doberman calm for 15 minutes or so before and after meals may help prevent the condition from developing.

One helpful technique is to let your dog's kibble soak in water for five minutes before you feed it to him. This causes the kibble to expand outside of his stomach, rather than inside. In addition, always keep your dog's water bowl full so he doesn't become so thirsty that he feels compelled to gulp down water when the bowl is finally filled.

Some antacid remedies made for human use contain an ingredient called simethicone, which can help slow or reduce the gas building up in a dog's stomach during a episode of bloat. Keep one of those products in your dog's first aid kit, so you'll have it immediately if your dog starts to bloat. It can be given to a Doberman Pinscher in the same dosage recommended for people. If you can slow down the expansion of gas in your dog's stomach, it may mean less pain for your dog and will give you more time to resolve the dangerous situation.

PARASITE CONTROL

Doberman Pinschers should be checked for internal parasites at least once a year. Young pups, elderly dogs, and unhealthy dogs all tend to build up large populations of various worms in the digestive tract. Worms seldom bother healthy, strong adults, but your Doberman should be checked and given deworming medicine, if needed. Your veterinarian will decide which worm medicine, and how much, your dog should have.

HEARTWORM: Heartworm is a serious health problem for dogs in most areas of the United States, but it's worst in moist, warm climates with large populations of mosquitoes. As its name suggests, heartworm is a worm that lives in the heart.

Mosquitoes carry heartworm. When a dog is infected with heartworm, a microscopic, immature stage of the heartworms (called microfilaria) circulates through the dog's bloodstream. If a mosquito bites the infected dog, along with its blood meal it draws in some microfilaria as well. If that mosquito bites another dog, some microfilaria will be injected into that new victim, where they will continue their life cycle and, in about three months, migrate into the heart itself and develop into adult worms. Within six to eight months, these adults begin to reproduce, adding more heartworms to the dog's growing load.

Each adult worm can reach a length of 12 inches (30.5 cm) or more. If a tangle of these worms clogs a dog's heart, it cannot pump efficiently, so the dog becomes weak and sick. A heavy load of heartworms, left untreated, will lead to the dog's death.

Administering prescription medications that kill the microfilaria before they develop into adult heartworms can prevent heartworm infection. The preventive must be used just before mosquitoes appear in spring until they go dormant for winter. In some parts of the country, mosquitoes stay active year round, so dogs must remain on preventive heartworm medication all year long. Your veterinarian can advise you on the best preventive regimen for your area.

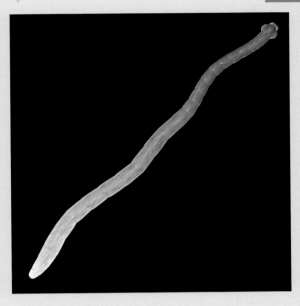

Parasitic worms can cause your Doberman Pinscher serious health problems.

Before dogs are given heartworm preventives, they must be tested to make sure they're not already infected. It can be fatal to administer preventive heartworm medication to a dog with adult heartworms. A different regimen is needed to clear up a heartworm infection. Because treating heartworm infection is dangerous, and sometimes fatal, it's much better to prevent infections from occurring.

FLEAS AND TICKS: External parasites like fleas also like dining on weakened animals, but they would not turn down a blood meal from any warm-blooded creature.

FAST FACT

External parasites like fleas and ticks seem to prefer dining on weakened individuals, but strong, healthy dogs are bothered by these parasites too.

Evidence of fleas on your Doberman Pinscher may include frequent scratching, chewing his rump at the base of his tail, or dark red or blackish "dirt" in that same area (that dirt is flea feces). If you see these signs, give your pet a flea bath as soon as possible.

Flea collars can help keep fleas away from your Doberman, and liquid anti-flea treatments, which are applied to the back of a dog's neck or withers, are also good. Veterinarians generally stock and dispense various brands of flea treatments, and several of these products are also available, without prescription, from pet supply stores and catalogs.

Another external parasite, the tick, is known to transmit a number of potentially devastating diseases to both dogs and humans, including Lyme disease. Ticks are small, flat parasites that burrow their tiny heads into their host's skin to subsist on blood. They are particularly attracted to the blood-rich skin of a dog's ears and face.

If there are ticks in your area, check your dog carefully for these "hitchhikers" after walks, especially if you've been out in brushy or grassy areas. If you find a tick on your Doberman, it should be removed as quickly as possible by grasping the tick close to the head with a pair of tweezers, then pulling it off. The longer a tick remains embedded in your dog's skin, the greater the chance it will transmit a tick-borne disease to your dog.

Ticks are nasty parasites that can transmit diseases to your Doberman Pinscher.

CHAPTER SEVEN

Things to Know As Your Puppy Grows

From six months to two years of age a Doberman Pinscher develops from an awkward, long-legged, adolescent into a graceful, well-proportioned adult. By one year of age, your Doberman will have attained most of his adult height, but he'll still be building muscle mass. Throughout this growing time, his food should be rich in highly digestible forms of protein and fat, as well as vitamins and minerals. These will ensure proper growth of muscle tissue, as well as high energy and overall good health.

Your Doberman's stomach is now large enough that he can be fed all the nutrition he needs in two meals a

Establishing a daily routine for your Doberman will make training easier.

day. If he enjoys a bedtime biscuit, he can certainly have that too. As long as he's eating the right food, not overindulging in treats, and getting plenty of exercise, you shouldn't have to worry that he's gaining too much weight. But if you notice your Doberman Pinscher is starting to get plump, cut back on the snacks.

It is easy to determine whether your dog is at a healthy weight. When he stands, look down at his back from above. You should be able to see a waist between your dog's last set of ribs and his hips. If there is little to no waistline, the dog is overweight. If you can see hip and spine bones clearly outlined through the fur, the dog is too thin.

When you look at your standing dog from the side, you should see a bit of tuck-up to the lower abdomen, just forward of the rear legs. If there is little to no tuck-up, the dog is overweight. If you can see the curve of every rib through the fur, the dog is too thin.

When you feel your dog's side with the tips of your fingers, you should be able to count his ribs without having to dig for them. If you can feel each rib with your fingertips, he is lean enough. Then run your flat palm along your dog's side. If it feels

TOO THIN OR TOO FAT?

Doberman Pinschers under two years old tend naturally to be on the lean side. This sometimes worries owners, but it is normal for the breed, as many Dobermans do not fill out with adult muscle until around three years of age. If your young adult Doberman is healthy and energetic but leaner than you'd like, he probably just hasn't reached maturity yet.

If your Doberman is thin enough to worry you, have your veterinarian examine him. If his lean body is normal for his age and development, your veterinarian will tell you. If she thinks he needs to gain weight, she will suggest healthy ways to accomplish that.

After Dobermans reach maturity they may become overweight if overfed or underexercised. Certain endocrine system abnormalities, such as diabetes or underactive thyroid, can cause excessive weight gain, even when owners are carefully watching the dog's diet. Your veterinarian can order laboratory tests if your dog's weight gain seems to be related to a larger health problem.

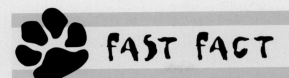

FAST FACT

Many dogs do better when their daily food allowance is divided into two portions and fed morning and evening, instead of feeding in one large meal.

firm and smooth, then he has enough flesh and muscle, but if you feel every rib against your hand, the dog is too thin.

In general, as far as health goes, a lean body in a dog is preferable to a fat one. It has been demonstrated, in numerous scientifically controlled experiments, that lean animals tend to have fewer chronic health problems and a longer lifespan than "normal weight" or slightly overweight individuals of the same species.

PROVIDING PROPER NUTRITION

Doberman Pinschers need to eat high-quality proteins to build and repair muscles, and keep their skin, organs, and blood healthy. Dogs use the fat in their diet as a main source of energy, so the quality and quantity of fat in their food is also important. Too much fat can cause loose stools and also tax the digestive system, especially the pancreas, yet too little fat is not healthy either. Kibble diets are generally high in carbohydrates

from grains or starchy vegetables like potatoes or peas. These carbohydrates can be used by the dog for energy but are not as easily digested as fats. A healthy diet must be readily digestible, nutritionally well balanced, and fed in the correct amount for the individual dog.

Most people feed their dogs commercial dry and canned foods. These vary in the quality of their ingredients, which is usually reflected in the price of the products. Cheaper foods often contain too much fat or vegetable protein, and this can lead to an unhealthy growth spurt. A high price does not guarantee excellence, though, so always read the ingredient list. Ideally, at least two of the first three ingredients should be meats. Your veterinarian should be able to help you pick a high-quality food

FAST FACT

An adult Doberman Pinscher needs to eat three to four cups of premium dry kibble or one and a half to two and a half pounds of fresh meat and bone each day. The amount will depend on your dog's size and activity level. Measure carefully to make sure he is eating the proper amount. Otherwise, your dog is likely to become overweight or obese.

that is made for large, active dogs like Doberman Pinschers.

There is a growing movement among dog owners to include fresh meat, bones, and vegetables in their dogs' diets. If you are interested in feeding your dog fresh foods instead of prepackaged foods, do some studying so you'll know how to provide balanced nutrition. There are a number of books available that describe healthy homemade diets for dogs. Also, check the Internet, as there are several good chat groups that discuss the benefits of fresh foods for dogs, either served raw or as part of a home-cooked diet. It's also a good idea to run homemade dietary plans past your veterinarian, as she can help ensure that your Doberman will be getting the nutrition he needs.

Dogs gain weight when they consume more food than they need for exercise and body maintenance. They lose weight if they burn more calories than they get from their food. This seems simple, but many dog owners do not recognize the importance of watching their dog's weight and adjusting his food intake accordingly. Few responsible dog owners would underfeed their dogs to unhealthy thinness, but many will overfeed their pets to a state of morbid obesity. Extra pounds on a dog steal years from his lifespan, so do not let your Doberman become obese.

VISITING THE VETERINARIAN

As an adult, your Doberman Pinscher should see the veterinarian at least once a year for a well-dog examination. In between these yearly examinations, if you notice anything that makes you suspect your Doberman Pinscher isn't fully healthy, consult your veterinarian immediately. An alert dog owner can help the veterinarian keep a dog healthy by noticing early signs of illness and seeking medical help before the problem worsens.

Some early signs of illness include decreases in energy and activity, different elimination habits, changes in appetite and water consumption, or uncharacteristic moodiness, grumpiness, or sensitivity to touch or sound. These kinds of changes don't necessarily mean your dog is sick, but they might, especially if you observe several suspicious signs within the same week.

Free running provides great exercise for your Doberman Pinscher. However, make sure your dog is in a safe area before you let him off his leash.

PROPER EXERCISE

By six months your Doberman Pinscher will be more than half his adult size and he'll have the energy of two adults. He'll need vigorous exercise every day. A walk around the block on a leash at your pace is not enough. In addition to daily walks, give your Doberman an opportunity to run free, preferably somewhere where there is room for him to stretch his legs.

Make sure that wherever you let your Doberman run for exercise is far away from traffic and other hazards. A galloping Doberman can travel very fast. Do not turn your pup loose in an unfenced area until he has been trained and comes when you call (see page 79–80). Until your Doberman follows your commands reliably, he will have to be content with exercising in safely fenced areas.

Your Doberman will probably enjoy playing catch in the backyard.

some other exercise that gives your Doberman Pinscher a good aerobic workout and lets him work all his muscles.

Regular exercise builds stamina and muscle condition without over-taxing the dog's strength or endurance. It is not healthy for a dog to sit idle all week, then exercise to exhaustion on the weekend. That all-or-nothing approach can result in strains, sprains, and other injuries that may be slow to heal. Lack of regular exercise leads to weakened muscles, including the heart. Insufficient exercise can also make a dog restless and irritable, which can lead to behavior problems like excessive barking, destructive chewing, overprotectiveness, or attempts to escape from your yard.

SOCIALIZATION

Socialization should not end when a pup isn't little any more. If your Doberman got a good start on social-

An adult Doberman Pinscher also needs daily exercise to stay healthy and maintain a positive mood. To stay fit, your adult Doberman Pinscher needs at least two brisk one-mile walks each day, plus 30 minutes or more of vigorous off-leash exercise like swimming, fetching, or running with dog pals.

For good exercise, there isn't much that can beat free-running play on soft ground with other dogs. This isn't always practical or possible, though, so it's important to provide

FAST FACT

Behavior acquired early in life is very durable. If you teach your Doberman puppy gentle games and polite manners, he will grow into a well-behaved adult.

A properly socialized Doberman Pinscher will be able to interact appropriately with other friendly dogs, such as this Fox Terrier.

izing when he was a youngster, keep building on that foundation. For best results, socialization activities must continue throughout your dog's life.

If you've just adopted an adolescent or adult Doberman Pinscher, and find that he has not been well socialized, it's important to help him catch up on his social skills. An adolescent or young adult Doberman that hasn't met many people or dogs will probably be somewhat shy.

Dobermans tend to hide uncertainty and fear behind a façade of loud barking or other aggressive behavior. A barking Doberman will be scary to many people and animals. Unfortunately, a Doberman that displays false bravado in this way can become so worked up that he bites the person or dog he has been barking at so fiercely.

If your Doberman reacts to someone or something in this way, the best thing you can do is to calmly walk him away from the "scary thing." Go far enough from the source of his fear that he no longer feels the need to flee or bark, and then just stand or sit there with him for a while and let him observe the "scary thing" from this safe distance. In a matter-of-fact tone of voice, describe what your Doberman is watching. Your calm tone of voice, your relaxed posture, and the increased distance from the scary thing will put your dog at ease and help him to understand that there is no reason to be afraid. Only reapproach scary things after your Doberman seems relaxed. You cannot force a fear to go away, but you can help it fade more quickly by making it seem less scary through your own calm reactions.

You may find that you need help working with an under-socialized Doberman Pinscher that behaves aggressively toward strange people or dogs. In this case, consult with a professional trainer, who may be able to help your Doberman overcome his fear.

TRAVELING WITH YOUR DOBERMAN

Doberman Pinschers love to be with their people and quickly become seasoned travelers. Following the tips below will make travel less stressful, both for you and for your pet.

Bringing your Doberman with you on regular short trips, such as running errands around the neighborhood, will make it easier to take him in the car on longer day trips or vacations.

AUTOMOBILE TRIPS: Most Dobermans enjoy car rides, and those that are used to short rides don't seem to mind longer trips at all. On a long road trip, most dogs enjoy the ever-changing scenery. Make sure to schedule regular stops where your Doberman can stretch, sniff around, and go to the bathroom. While driving, make sure your dog is securely fastened, either with a dog seatbelt harness, in his crate, or behind a vehicle barrier.

When traveling, plan your overnight accommodations in advance. Not all hotels or motels will accept pets. Look for establishments that claim to be "pet friendly," and make sure to ask whether there will be extra fees to allow your dog to stay in the room. Such establishments can be found online at Web sites like PetsWelcome.com, PetTravel.com, and LetsGoPets.com.

Pack a travel bag for your Doberman that includes food, bowls, toys, treats, any medication he needs, and a first-aid kit. You should also bring his bed or an old blanket for him to sleep on, identification tags, and his leash. If you'll be vacationing with your Doberman far from home, have a special ID tag made that includes your local phone number or a cell phone number. This way you can be reached if your pet wanders off and gets lost.

AIRPLANE RIDES: It's usually easier and more pleasant for dogs to travel by automobile than by airplane. Medium-sized and large dogs traveling by plane must be transported in a crate in the cargo hold of a jet, and this can be a scary and stressful experience. However, Dobermans that have flown a few times will usually settle into their flight crates calmly.

When booking your flight, ask whether the airline has any special program for transporting live animals. At least one airline has a special program for flying animals in cargo, and their baggage handlers have been specially trained to handle live animals. Also, ask whether there are any factors that you need to consider when bringing your Doberman along. The airline will probably want to see a health certificate from your veterinarian, and may have other requirements as well. Allow enough

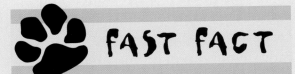

FAST FACT

Most Dobermans like car rides so much that, if you leave your car door open in the driveway, you may find your Doberman snoozing on the back seat, waiting for a ride.

time to gather all necessary paperwork before your flight date.

If you are traveling to Hawaii, or to countries outside the United States, be sure you know all the animal regulations for your destination. Most out-of-country destinations do not permit pets to enter without proper documentation and immunizations. Some countries require animals to be quarantined for a lengthy period in a government-approved boarding kennel.

Web sites like Petflight.com provide information about traveling with pets on various airlines, as well as helpful tips about traveling by air.

LEAVING YOUR DOBERMAN AT HOME

There are times you may have to travel without your Doberman, such as on a business trip. When you must leave your pal behind, there are several care alternatives to choose from.

If you have friends or relatives who are willing to take good care of your dog, you might be able to leave him with them or have them come stay at your home. That would be a great solution.

However, many people don't have friends or relatives able or willing to take on that responsibility. In that case, there are pet sitters for hire who will visit your Doberman Pinscher two or more times a day, feeding, exercising, grooming, and even medicating the dog, if necessary. Some pet sitters will stay overnight at your home and care for your pets almost the way you would. They charge more for that kind of service, but for some dog owners—especially those with multiple pets—whatever the overnight sitter charges is worth the cost.

If you're traveling, or even if you're just away from home for long days all week and find that you don't have much time or energy to exercise your dog when you get home, consider doggie day care. At day care facilities, dogs are dropped off in the morning and picked up later the same day. Some day care centers have vans to pick up the dogs and take them home, saving the owners that trouble.

Keep in mind that dogs with aggressive attitudes toward either

If you don't have a family member or friend who can take care of your Doberman Pinscher when you're out of town, consider hiring a pet sitter. Organizations like Pet Sitters International (www.petsit.com; pictured at right) or the National Association of Professional Pet Sitters (www.petsitters.org) are a great place to begin your search.

people or other dogs are not good candidates for doggie day care. It will be stressful for them to be around strange humans and dogs all day, and they will escalate the stress level of everyone else, both human and canine. Dogs that get along well with others can have a lot of fun at day care, however. Dogs that like people but not other dogs may enjoy being walked, petted, and played with by the staff.

Boarding kennels are mainly for overnight stays, though many offer doggie day care as well. Most boarding kennels keep the dogs in runs or cages most of the time, walking them on-leash for a bit of exercise or turning them out into a fenced area to walk around and sniff on their own. A Doberman Pinscher that dislikes other dogs may not do well at a kennel, unless his run is blocked visually from a view of other dogs. A dog that isn't good with people may fare well at some kennels, but it depends on how skilled the staff is in dealing with that type of dog.

CHAPTER EIGHT

Training Your Doberman Pinscher

You should have started teaching your puppy good manners and obedience the day you brought him home. This training will continue for the rest of his life. Dogs learn the rules of life by paying attention to what works and what doesn't, so you're training your Doberman Pinscher every time you interact with him.

When your Doberman Pinscher is three or four months old, he can be enrolled in an obedience school. Training classes will teach him that wonderful things come to good dogs that do as they're told. If you wait until your Doberman Pinscher is six months or older, he'll be harder to train, because he'll think he knows how life works.

Your Doberman will obey if you are fair, calm, and consistent in your training.

To find a reputable trainer, ask for recommendations from your veterinarian and your friends who own dogs. Training classes can be a lot of fun if you like the instructor and her methods. When you get some leads on trainers near you, call each one and ask about their experiences with large strong dogs like Doberman Pinschers. If a trainer seems to feel "right," make arrangements to observe a class without your dog, so you'll see how the trainer relates to both two-legged and four-legged students.

Some Doberman Pinscher owners prefer to train their dogs themselves. You can train a dog to do just about anything you'd like, but initially you should focus on some basic obedience commands: sit, down, stay, and come. These commands will provide a foundation for any other type of training you have in mind.

SIT: Sitting is such a natural position for dogs that your Doberman may adopt this position on his own. If you reward him with praise or treats each time he sits, and eventually add the "sit" command, you can teach your dog to sit at your whim. If your dog can't figure things out quite this easily, you can help him into the sit position by holding a treat above his head, just behind his eye level. When he looks up to keep his eyes on the treat, his back end may naturally drop into a sit. If not, you can further assist your dog by scooping his back legs underneath him. Plenty of repetition and generous rewards when he gets it right will soon have your dog sitting at your direction.

Part of being consistent is using the same command word or phrase every time you want your dog to do something. If you tell him to "sit" one week, "sit down," the next, and "sit, boy" the following, you'll confuse your Doberman.

Using treats as rewards will help your dog learn to drop into the "down" position at your command.

DOWN: You can teach your dog to lie down on command by starting from the sit position. Hold a treat on the floor in front of your dog and slowly pull it away from him. This will encourage your dog to stretch out his head and front feet as he tries to keep his nose close to the treat. If your dog stretches out even a little bit, reward him with the treat. Even if your dog has not yet reached a full down position, you should reward any movement he makes in the right direction, as many obedi-ence skills are best taught in small increments.

If your dog stands up or gets out of position, put him back into a sit and start over. A lot of patience, combined with small enough "baby steps," will eventually result in the desired behavior. Then, you can begin using the "down" command so your dog can learn to associate this word with the correct position.

STAY: The "stay" command is very useful for controlling the movement of your dog, especially in situations where safety is a concern. This command involves two components—distance and duration—that must be taught in increments. You can work on both at the same time, provided you take this training slow.

With your dog in a sitting position, tell him to "stay," take one step away from him, and then step toward him immediately. If your dog has maintained his sitting position, reward him. Repeat this a couple times. When your dog remains seated consistently when you take one step away, you can start moving two steps away, and repeat the process. Gradually increase both the distance and the duration. If your Doberman Pinscher breaks his stay at any point, it's an indication that you're expecting too much too fast. Back up a few steps and progress more slowly.

The stay command will become a little more challenging for your dog when you are ready to practice out-of-sight stays. Your dog likes to know where you are at all times, and the minute you step out of the room, he'll attempt to follow you. Set your dog up for success by stepping out of the room for only a fraction of a second in the beginning. Return immediately to reward your dog. This way, your dog will learn that you fully intend to come back, and he'll be a little more patient in waiting for longer periods of time.

COME: The "come" command is the most important skill you can teach your Doberman Pinscher. A dog that

Your Doberman Pinscher should not be allowed off his leash in public until he has learned to come reliably when he's called.

does not come when called is an accident waiting to happen. That's why you should practice "come" every chance you get. Keep some treats in your pocket and call your dog from different rooms in your house at different times of the day. Call your dog only once each time and reward him whenever he responds. If he doesn't come on the first call, he gets no reward.

You can practice "come" outdoors in a fenced area or on a long leash, but again, only call your dog once each time and only reward your dog when he responds immediately. Don't force your dog to come to you by pulling on his leash, or he will believe that "come" is only mandatory when he's on a leash. Instead, coax your dog to you by calling him in a happy voice or running a few steps away from him to encourage him to chase you.

The whole purpose of practicing the "come" command constantly is to condition your dog to respond automatically, without thinking about it, so that he will eventually listen to you even in the face of distractions. The "come" should always be presented in an upbeat manner, because if you scold or punish your dog when he doesn't come immediately, he won't be in much of a hurry to come to you the next time!

ADVANCED TRAINING

If you enjoyed teaching your pup the basics, you'll probably enjoy teaching him advanced skills even more. As your dog becomes better trained, you may want to prepare him for fun activities that you can do together, such as dog shows and competitions.

CONFORMATION: Conformation shows are competitive events where Doberman Pinschers and purebred dogs of other breeds are judged against the written Standard of Perfection for their breed. The standard describes the ideal appearance, gait, and temperament of the breed. Males and females are judged separately, and the winner in each sex is awarded from one to five championship points. The number of points

FAST FACT

Show grooming for a Doberman Pinscher is really no different from ordinary day-to-day grooming. Some breeds take all day to get ready for the show ring, but a bath, a thorough brushing, and a nail trim are all a Doberman Pinscher usually requires. A show dog's nails must be maintained quite short, so trimming them once a week is a good idea.

is determined by how many dogs competed. Winners in both sexes are then judged together, and one dog is selected as the Best of Breed (BOB) for that day.

The Best of Breed winner goes on to compete with the other BOB winners from his breed's group. The American Kennel Club places Doberman Pinschers in the Working group, which means that he'll be competing against other Working dogs, such as the Boxer, Great Dane, Rottweiler, and Siberian Husky, to name a few. The winning dog in the Working group will compete against the winners of the other six AKC groups—Herding, Hound, Non-Sporting, Sporting, Terrier, and Toy—for the title of Best in Show.

A Conformation dog must be kept in the peak of health in order to win. Your Doberman Pinscher's muscles should be well developed and firm, his eyes should be bright and clear, his nails should be short, his coat should shine, and his teeth must be pearly white. Conformation dogs

To succeed as show dogs, Doberman Pinschers must conform closely to the breed standard.

are trained to pose ("stack") for presentation and examination by the judge. Doberman Pinschers are posed with legs foursquare and hind legs stretched back slightly. This pose shows off the desired angulation of the Doberman Pinscher's front and rear quarters. They are also trained to trot slowly around the ring so that the judge can evaluate their gait, or the way they move.

A show dog must allow himself to be handled all over by a stranger (the judge), who will examine your Doberman Pinscher's mouth, teeth, and, for males, the testicles. In the

THE COSTS OF COMPETITION

If you decide to get involved in competitive sports with your Doberman Pinscher, the annual cost of owning your dog will rise as you add on the following expenses:

Entry fees: $20 to $40 for each class entered. Depending on which sports and how many you compete in with your dog, entry fees for one show or trial can run from $20 to $100, or more.

Transportation: Fuel for your car or motor home to drive to shows within driving distance, and plane fare for important shows farther from home, such as the Doberman Pinscher Club of America's annual National Specialty show.

Lodging: Hotel or motel rooms range from $80 to several hundred dollars a night, depending on quality, location, and whether or not the pet fee charged by the hotel is refundable. At some events, participants are permitted to camp on the show grounds. If you own a motor home or camping trailer, this option usually costs from $15 to $60 a night.

Meals away from home: Budget appropriately, depending on your appetite and tastes as well as where you're going.

Handler's fees: $100 to $600 or more per show. Hiring a professional handler to exhibit your Doberman Pinscher in Conformation events, instead of handling him yourself, can increase your dog's success in the show ring, but the cost of earning those awards will increase as well.

Photographs of wins: When your Doberman wins at a show, captures a title, or earns a perfect score, you will want to get a photograph to remember the day. Sponsoring clubs arrange to have one or more professional photographers on site at the show to provide that service to exhibitors. Dog show photographers generally charge between $25 and $35 per print.

conformation ring, the judge evaluates both temperament and physique for conformance to the Standard of Perfection.

OBEDIENCE: Obedience trials may be held in conjunction with Conformation shows or as stand-alone events. Obedience trials test a dog's response to his handler. The dog must obey verbal commands and hand signals immediately, precisely, and willingly. The handler is allowed to command the dog once, and then must give no further cues until the exercise is complete. Between exercises, the handler is allowed to praise and pet the dog, but the dog must remain under control.

There are several levels of difficulty in Obedience, with a title to be earned at each level by attaining three to ten qualifying scores at that level. A qualifying score in Obedience is 170 or better. A perfect score is 200.

Novice Obedience requires the dog to heel close to his handler's left side, both on-leash and off-leash, as he walks, turns, halts, and changes speeds as directed by the judge. The dog must stay when told, then come when called and sit facing the handler within easy reach. Each dog must do an individual stand-stay, allowing the judge to touch him, and

Obedience trials are meant to showcase dogs that have been trained to behave in the home, in public places, and in the presence of other dogs. At the novice level, dogs must perform exercises both on-leash and off-leash. Higher levels of Obedience competition include more challenging exercises. Information about Obedience can be found online at www.akc.org/events/obedience/getting_started.cfm

FAST FACT

Put your Doberman's basic obedience skills into practice at mealtimes by making him sit politely and telling him when he can proceed with his meal. This not only reinforces that you are in charge, it will also get him started eating calmly, which reduces the likelihood of bloat.

then they all perform sit and down stays together, for one and three minutes, respectively. Three qualifying scores at the Novice level earn the Companion Dog (CD) title.

The next level is Open, where the dog must heel a pattern off-leash as the judge directs. There are jumps and retrieving exercises in Open, and for the group sit and down stays, the handlers must leave their dogs and wait out of sight for three and five minutes, respectively. Three qualifying scores in Open earn the Companion Dog Excellent (CDX) title.

The next advanced level in Obedience is called Utility. Here the handler does a silent signal exercise, cueing the dog to sit, down, stand, stay, and come, using only hand signals. There is a send-out, where the dog must run the handler to the far end of the ring, turn, and sit facing

the handler, waiting to be signaled which of two jumps he must leap on the way back in. In a directed retrieve in Utility, the judge designates which of three cotton work gloves the handler will send the dog to fetch.

Utility events also include a scent discrimination exercise. This requires matching sets of five metal articles and five leather articles. These can be dumbbell-shaped articles manufactured for Obedience training or common objects made of those materials, in sets of five identical items. (For example, five identical leather moccasins and five identical metal tablespoons may be used.) The objects are numbered, then placed on the floor at the other end of the ring, after the handler holds one for a few moments to scent it. On the judge's signal, the handler sends the dog to find the scented item. The dog sniffs the pile of objects and retrieves the correct one. An item of the other material is then scented by the handler and placed among the remaining articles. The dog must find that second scented item and carry it to the handler.

Three qualifying scores in Utility earn a competitor the Utility Dog (UD) title. Dogs can earn the Utility Dog Excellent (UDX) title by earning qualifying scores in both Open and Utility classes at the same trial, and by doing that ten times.

RALLY: In this sport the dog and handler heel together around a course of numbered stations, each with a sign indicating an exercise for the handler and the dog to perform. Each of more than fifty exercises tests the dog and handler's teamwork skills. In Rally the handler is permitted to talk to and encourage the dog as much as she wants. The handler is allowed to praise the dog, but not pet him, both while performing the exercises and when moving between them.

Novice-level Rally is performed on-leash. Advanced and Excellent Rally levels are performed off-leash. A perfect score in AKC Rally is 100. Titles are earned at each level with three qualifying scores of 70 or higher. The titles are Rally Novice (RN), Rally Advanced (RA), and Rally Excellent (RE). Another title, the Rally Advanced Excellent (RAE), can be earned after completing the RE. This additional title requires the team to earn qualifying scores in both Advanced and Excellent classes at the same trial, and to do that ten times.

Some Rally exercises are similar to Obedience exercises—sits, downs, stays, call-fronts, finishes-to-heel, stands, and figure-8s. There are also challenging exercises not used in Obedience, requiring the dog to heel through serpentines and elongated spirals. There are many different turns in Rally, including 90° and 180° turns, as encountered in Obedience, and 270° and 360° turns to both left and right.

In Rally, the judge only tells the team when to start. From then on, the handler guides herself and her dog around the ring, following the course without direction from the judge. The team moves from sign to sign in numbered order, performing each one as described in the regulations.

Gentleness on the part of the handler and willingness on the part of the dog are hallmarks of an exemplary Rally team. Everything a dog and handler do from the moment they enter the Rally ring gate until they leave the ring after their run affects their score. Handler mistakes—such as guiding the dog with a tight leash, making collar-jerk cor-

FAST FACT

Training in Rally will often improve a dog's attitude and make him more attentive to commands in everyday life.

rections, or speaking sharply to the dog—or dog mistakes, like being uncooperative getting into start position, can lose points for the team before they even start the course.

When the handler and dog are at the start sign, the judge asks, "Are you ready?" The handler checks her dog to be sure he's in position beside her, and then replies to the judge, "Yes," or "Ready." The judge then says, "Forward," and, from there on, says nothing more. The judge silently follows behind or to the side of the team at a distance and angle that provides the best view of each station. The judge scores the team's performance as they proceed from sign to sign, doing each exercise along the course.

The handler may speak to and encourage the dog as much as she wants. Repeated cues and signals are not penalized, and if the team cannot successfully perform an exercise on their first attempt, a retry is allowed. The retry costs the team three points off their final score, but if the retry is successful, that three-point deduction is less "expensive" than losing a full ten points for incorrectly performing the station.

AGILITY: This sport is judged on speed and accuracy over a course of jumps, tunnels, ramps, and other

Doberman Pinschers have the speed and athletic ability to be successful in Agility competitions. Here, a Doberman leaps over a 24-inch hurdle.

A Doberman Pinscher practices running over an A-frame.

obstacles. Each dog is timed as he individually races over a numbered obstacle course, as directed by his handler. In Agility, the dog performs the jumps and obstacles and the handler does not. The handler may run with the dog, directing him from up close, or may direct him from behind or to the side at a greater distance.

The experienced Agility dog learns to respond instantly on the course to subtle movements of his handler's shoulders, hips, and knees as cues for changes in direction or pace. Most handlers also use hand signals and verbal cues to give their dogs specific information, like which one of two side-by-side obstacles to tackle. Handlers may also talk, clap, praise, and verbally encourage the dog, but may not touch the dog or any of the obstacles.

In Agility, a dog can earn titles at the Novice, Open, and Advanced levels by earning three qualifying scores for each level. First-place through fourth-place ribbons are awarded to the dogs with the fewest faults and the fastest run times. Dogs compete for placements only against other dogs of their same approximate height. A dog can earn titles without placing.

All the jumps on a course are set at a height appropriate for each competitor. Tall dogs have higher jumps than short dogs, which helps make Agility fair for all. To determine the proper jump height division for your dog, a judge at an Agility trial will measure him at the withers and issue a height card with his official measurement. Jumps are adjusted from four inches (10 cm) high to 24 inches (61 cm) or more. The average Doberman Pinscher stands from 24 to 28 inches tall, so they will typically have 24 or 26 inch (61 or 66 cm) jumps in AKC Agility events. Only the jumps are adjusted for each dog's height; the other obstacles stay the same for all dogs.

AKC Agility classes include Standard, in which the contestants cover a course that uses all possible obstacles, and Jumpers with Weaves, in which the course only includes jumps and weave poles. There is now also a challenging course, the FAST class, where the handler directs his dog over part of the course from a distance. Other organizations offer Agility contests similar to those sanctioned by the American Kennel Club, as well as contests that are different.

SERVICE AND THERAPY DOGS

Doberman Pinschers have proven their merit in the work world as well as the sport arena. Well-trained Dobermans can make reliable Service Dogs (also called Assistance Dogs), and can do many tasks for disabled humans that would otherwise require hiring a human helper. Mobility assistance dogs can carry groceries, retrieve dropped or distant items, pull wheelchairs, help a person get in and out of bed, help the person dress and undress, fetch drinks from a refrigerator, open and close heavy doors, and other helpful tasks.

Doberman Pinschers have long served as guide dogs to the blind. Guide dogs are trained to safely lead blind individuals through public places. A guide dog learns to recognize and avoid situations that might endanger his blind partner. Normally, when the person commands the dog to move forward, that's what the dog will immediately do. However, if the dog is commanded to do anything that could endanger his partner, he will refuse to move.

The Doberman Pinschers' strength and high intelligence make these dogs well suited to police work.

Doberman Pinschers can also serve as hearing-assistance dogs. These dogs are trained to alert their deaf or hearing-impaired human partner to important sounds, like the person's name, a baby's cry, an alarm clock's ring, an oven timer's buzz, and a fire alarm's wail. When the dog hears the sound, he goes to the person and gives a signal, such as a nudge with his nose, indicating that he has heard something the person needs to know about. Once the hearing dog gets the person's attention, he will indicate the source of the sound, so the person can respond to it.

Usually, Service Dogs are selected or bred for their job, then trained by professionals to perform the needed tasks.

Many Dobermans participate in pet-assisted therapy, visiting nursing homes and other care facilities. They

Detailed information about service dog training and therapy pet work can be found online. Check the Web site of the Delta Society, www.deltasociety.org (pictured) or Therapy Dogs International (www.tdi-dog.org).

bring residents the joy and unconditional affection that only a dog can give. Some Doberman Pinschers serve as emotional therapy dogs, helping patients to open up to something outside themselves and begin to heal. Sometimes traumatized individuals who have become unable to speak or relate to human beings can find comfort and safety in the non-judgmental affection of a gentle, well-behaved Doberman Pinscher. If you enjoy sharing your Doberman Pinscher's loving nature with others, and if he is socialized and well behaved in public, consider getting involved with local volunteers who do pet-assisted therapy visits.

CANINE GOOD CITIZEN

The American Kennel Club's Canine Good Citizen (CGC) Test is open to dogs of all breeds, as well as mixes. This CGC Test involves ten exercises that test the dog's social and obedience skills. To pass, your dog must show that he can:

- Accept a friendly stranger
- Sit politely while being petted
- Allow grooming and examination
- Walk on a loose lead

- Walk through a crowd
- Sit and lie down on command, and stay in place
- Come when called
- Behave politely around other dogs
- React confidently to distractions, such as sudden loud noises; and
- Maintain his good manners when you leave him with another person

Dogs that pass the CGC Test are issued certificates touting that achievement. The benefits of CGC certification go beyond the obvious one of having a well-behaved dog. Some homeowner's insurance companies require CGC certification before they insure owners of certain breeds. Some communities are considering lowering the license fees for dogs that have earned CGC certificates, and some landlords will reduce, or even waive, their standard pet deposit for CGC dogs.

The Kennel Club of the United Kingdom runs a similar training program called the Good Citizen Dog Scheme.

TEMPERAMENT TESTING

Local and regional dog clubs around the United States holds temperament Evaluation Tests. At these events, a trained evaluator observes each dog in turn as they go through a series of structured exercises. Dogs of any breed can take the test.

The exercises present specific situations, such as a friendly stranger, a threatening stranger, the startling opening of an umbrella, the sound of gunfire, and more. The evaluator scores the dog on courage, protectiveness, and other qualities of temperament.

A dog that can pass all parts of the Temperament Test with high marks possesses the proper temperament for a working Doberman Pinscher. Those that pass receive a certificate and are permitted to add the initials "TT" (Temperament Tested) after their name, to signify their achievement.

CHAPTER NINE

Caring for Your Senior Doberman Pinscher

As your Doberman ages, his body will go through gradual changes, both externally and internally. His digestive system slows down and becomes less efficient, and his metabolism may slow too. The heart gradually weakens, as do other muscles. Tumors, cysts, and other growths may appear. His hearing and eyesight will start to fail. Health problems like cancer, heart disease, diabetes, stroke, and nerve disorders plague senior dogs, just as they do senior humans.

On average, a Doberman Pinscher can live for 10 to 13 years or more. Dobermans are considered "seniors" at around eight years old.

It is natural for your Doberman Pinscher to have less energy as he ages.

There are no cures for aging, but there are ways make your Doberman Pinscher's senior years more comfortable.

NUTRITION

As a dog ages, his digestive system often becomes less efficient, making it more important than ever that proteins and fats he consumes are high quality and easily digested. Most senior dogs exercise less than they did when younger, so it is often necessary to reduce the senior dog's caloric intake to prevent weight gain. An older dog in good health can maintain the proper weight eating the same type of food he has always eaten, but the serving size must be reduced to match his lower metabolism and activity level.

Some senior dogs develop digestive or metabolic problems. For these dogs it may not be enough to simply reduce the size of their meals; they'll need a completely different

As your Doberman Pinscher ages, the hairs on his muzzle and chest will probably begin to turn grey.

diet. Ask your veterinarian to help you find the best way to keep your senior dog's weight under control and make sure he receives the nutrients he needs for optimal health.

If your senior Doberman develops heart, liver, or kidney problems, he'll probably need a special diet. Prescription diets, available from veterinarians, are formulated specifically to help dogs stay as healthy as possible despite impaired organ function.

FAST FACT

Dogs can live healthy lives without consuming many carbohydrates because the canine digestive system utilizes fats for the body's energy needs.

EXERCISE

Your senior Doberman still needs regular daily exercise to keep his heart, lungs, and muscles healthy and working properly. Lack of exercise will cause muscles, including the heart, to weaken and deteriorate, and an inactive dog will become overweight. The combination of weakness and weight gain will lead to a greater tendency toward inactivity, sending your pet pal into a downward spiral of worsening health.

You can avoid this unhealthy situation by keeping your Doberman active as he ages. Obviously, your senior Doberman shouldn't go mountain climbing or swimming in whitewater rapids, even if he did these types of activities easily when he was younger. Instead, make sure that your senior dog receives moderate daily exercise. A daily walk or a 15-minute game of fetch will keep his heart, lungs, and muscles in good condition. Never exer-

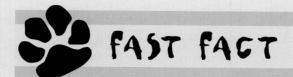

FAST FACT

A Doberman Pinscher's short coat may not be enough to keep the dog warm and dry outdoors in very cold or wet weather. A water resistant vest or coat will help him stay comfortable on winter walks and outings.

cise your senior Doberman to exhaustion, and be willing, as he ages, to allow your walks to become slower.

HEALTH ISSUES

As a senior, your Doberman Pinscher should see the veterinarian every six months. The vet will look for signs of a serious health problem, such as cancer, in your dog.

The best way to detect cancer early is to be alert to any changes in your dog's body or health that might indicate something is not right. As you pet your Doberman, gently explore his body with your fingers. Lumps, bumps, and slow-to-heal sores sometimes indicate cancer. If

Many treats are higher in calories than regular foods. Be sure to include the calories from treats when determining your Doberman's daily food intake.

Even if he's slowing down, your senior Doberman will still enjoy taking walks with you.

Senior Doberman Pinschers are likely to develop hearing and vision problems as they age. But even if your dog loses his hearing or vision, he may still function quite well, as his other senses will compensate somewhat for the loss.

you feel something unusual, watch that spot for a week. The veterinarian should investigate any sores that do not heal within a week despite cleaning and care, or lumps that do not go away in that time.

Bad breath can originate from dirty teeth, but it can also indicate health problems, including cancer of internal organs. Foul breath that comes and goes is not unusual, but if your Doberman's breath begins to

always smell bad, have the veterinarian examine him. If the doctor suspects anything beyond indigestion, she may have him tested for more serious health problems.

There are many types of cancer, and some are more deadly than others. Different cancers are treated with different types of medical intervention. Treatment may include surgical removal of tumors, radiation, and chemotherapy. Dietary supplements may be prescribed to strengthen general health both during and after treatments. Some types of cancers, when detected early, have a good prognosis for successful treatment and recovery.

INCONTINENCE

Incontinence of bladder and bowels is a problem that occurs with many dogs in their senior years. Medication can help some cases of incontinence, but not all. It's important to help your senior Doberman maintain his dignity. Incontinence can make that challenging, because most incontinent dogs are aware that they are soiling themselves and your floors. Your dog will feel frustrated and ashamed, so disguise your own frustration with the mess and treat your dog with as much respect as possible.

Do your best to keep your incontinent dog clean, so his skin isn't scalded by urine. You will need to change his bedding every time he soils it. One way to cut down on laundry is to keep a doggie diaper on your incontinent Doberman. This must be changed numerous times a day, but that is still less work than doing multiple loads of laundry.

SAYING GOODBYE

Nothing lasts forever—at least nothing mortal does. Eventually the time

In addition to physical changes, expect your senior Doberman Pinscher's behavior and personality to change as well. Older dogs are more likely to become anxious when separated from their owners. The barking, whining, and destructive behavior that occurred when he was a puppy may recur suddenly during the senior years. Be patient and loving during this time in your dog's life.

Looking at photos of you and your Doberman in happier times can help ease the pain of his passing.

will come that you and your beloved Doberman Pinscher must say good-bye to each other. This is a sad time, as you think back to all the good times and some of the rough spots you have traveled together. Your dog is not alone in his aging—you have aged too, though his dog-years have run out before your human-years.

When you know your Doberman's time is getting close, there are some things you can do to ease this final transition for you both.

• Take some new photographs of your Doberman. If possible, visit a few of the places that hold good memories and have a friend photograph you and your dog together there.

- Write your feelings in a journal. Jot down disjointed thoughts or form your words into poetry. Either way, expressing yourself through writing will help you to release some of the emotions you are probably feeling.

- Pick a special spot where you will bury your dog's remains or scatter his ashes. Take your dog there, if possible, and share a picnic, so the spot holds a memory of a pleasant time together.

- Have a party for your dog and invite the people who care deeply for both of you. They deserve an opportunity to say goodbye too. Let people share their memories and feelings about your Doberman. Tape record or video that sharing time—it may be very healing for you to listen to or watch the tape in the months after your dog passes.

FAST FACT

The actual process of euthanasia is painless for the dog. The vet will usually administer a sedative first, so your friend will fall asleep. Then an overdose of anesthesia is administered, and the dog's heart simply stops beating.

Your dog may pass away in his sleep, or he may cling stubbornly to this world. As our dogs' best friends and lifelong caregivers we have the option to provide a final kindness to our dogs—a painless passing. If your Doberman is suffering in his last days, talk over that final option with your veterinarian and decide whether that will be the right action to take.

And when you and your Doberman say your final goodbye for this lifetime, comfort yourself knowing you've loved your old friend in life, and in death, the best ways you could.

Organizations to Contact

American Animal Hospital Association
12575 West Bayaud Ave.
Lakewood, CO 80228
Phone: 303-986-2800
Fax: 800-252-2242
E-mail: info@aahanet.org
Web site: www.aahanet.org

American Canine Association, Inc.
P.O. Box 808
Phoenixville, PA 19460
Phone: 800-651-8332
Fax: 800-422-1864
E-mail: acacanines@aol.com
Web site: www.acainfo.com

American Dog Breeders Assn.
P.O. Box 1771
Salt Lake City, UT 84110
Phone: 801-936-7513
E-mail: bstofshw@adba.cc
Web site: www.adbadogs.com

American Humane Association
63 Inverness Dr. East
Englewood, CO 80112
Phone: 303-792-9900
Fax: 303-792-5333
Web site: www.americanhumane.org

American Kennel Club
8051 Arco Corporate Dr., Suite 100
Raleigh, NC 27617
Phone: 919-233-9767
E-mail: info@akc.org
Web site: www.akc.org

Association of Pet Dog Trainers
150 Executive Center Dr., Box 35
Greenville, SC 29615
Phone: 800-738-3647
E-mail: information@apdt.com
Web site: www.apdt.com

The Canadian Kennel Club
89 Skyway Avenue, Suite 100
Etobicoke, Ontario, M9W 6R4
Canada
Phone: 416-675-5511
E-mail: information@ckc.ca
Web site: www.ckc.ca/en

Canine Eye Registration Foundation
1717 Philo Road
P.O. Box 3007
Urbana, IL 61803-3007
Phone: 217-693-4800
E-mail: cerf@vmdb.org
Web site: www.vmdb.org/cerf.html

**Canine Health
Foundation**
P.O. Box 37941
Raleigh, NC 27627-7941
Phone: 888-682-9696
Fax: 919-334-4011
E-mail: akcchf@akc.org
Web site: www.akcchf.org

Delta Society
875 124th Ave., NE
Suite 101
Bellevue, WA 98005
Phone: 425-226-7357
E-mail: info@deltasociety.org
Web site: www.deltasociety.org

**Doberman Pinscher Club
of America**
3345 Musgrave Rd.
Williamsburg, OH 45176
E-mail:
    DPCApubliceducation@dpca.org
Web-site: www.dpca.org

**Doberman Pinscher Club of
Canada**
Linda Hill, secretary
39 Edgeford Rd NW
Calgary, AB T3A 2S5
Canada
Phone: 403-698-1917
E-mail: secretary@dpcc.ca
Web site: www.dpcc.ca

**The Dobermann Club
of the United Kingdom**
Mrs Jackie Ingram, secretary
Foxburrows, Beredens Lane
Great Warley,
Brentwood, Essex
CM13 3JB
United Kingdom
Phone: 01277-260457
E-mail:
    jojavik_dobermanns@hotmail.com
Web site:
    www.thedobermannclub.co.uk

**Humane Society
of the United States**
2100 L St., NW
Washington, DC 20037
Phone: 202-452-1100
Fax: 301-548-7701
Email: info@hsus.org
Web site: www.hsus.org

**The Kennel Club
of the United Kingdom**
1-5 Clarges St.
Picadilly
London
W1J 8AB
United Kingdom
Phone: 0870 606 6750
Fax: 020 7518 1058
Web site: www.thekennelclub.org.uk

National Association of Dog Obedience Instructors
PMB 369
729 Grapevine Hwy
Hurst, TX 76054-2085
E-mail: corrsec2@nadoi.org
Web site: www.nadoi.org

National Association of Professional Pet Sitters (NAPPS)
17000 Commerce Parkway, Suite C
Mt. Laurel, NJ 08054
Phone: 856-439-0324
E-mail: napps@ahint.com
Web site: www.petsitters.org

National Dog Registry
P.O. Box 51105
Mesa, AZ 85208
Phone: 800-NDR-DOGS
Web site: www.nationaldogregistry.com

North American Dog Agility Council (NADAC)
P.O. Box 1206
Colbert, OK 74733
E-mail: info@nadac.com
Web site: www.nadac.com

North American Flyball Association (NAFA)
1400 West Devon Ave., #512
Chicago, IL 60660
Phone: 800-318-6312
Web site: www.flyball.org

Orthopedic Foundation for Animals (OFA)
2300 East Nifong Boulevard
Columbia, MO 65201
Phone: 573-442-0418
Web site: www.offa.org

Pet Industry Joint Advisory Council
1220 19th Street, NW Suite 400
Washington, DC 20036
Phone: 202-452-1525
E-mail: info@pijac.org
Web site: www.pijac.org

Pet Loss Support Hotline
College of Veterinary Medicine
Cornell University
Ithaca, NY 14853-6401
Phone: 607-253-3932
Web site: www.vet.cornell.edu/
public/petloss

Pet Sitters International (PSI)
201 East King Street
King, NC 27021-9161
Phone: 336-983-9222
Fax: 336-983-9222
E-mail: info@petsit.com
Web site: www.petsit.com

Therapy Dogs International, Inc.
88 Bartley Road
Flanders, NJ 07836
Phone: 973-252-9800
Web site: www.tdi-dog.org

UK National Pet Register
74 North Albert Street, Dept 2
Fleetwood, Lancasterhire
FY7 6BJ
United Kingdom
Web site: www.nationalpetregister.org

**United States Dog Agility
Association, Inc. (USDAA)**
P.O. Box 850955
Richardson, TX 75085-0955
Phone: 972-487-2200
Fax: 972-272-4404
Web site: www.usdaa.com

Veterinary Medical Databases
1717 Philo Rd.
Urbana, IL 61803-3007
Phone: 217-693-4800
E-mail: cerf@vmdb.org
Web site: www.vmdb.org

**World Canine Freestyle
Organization (WCFO)**
PO Box 350122
Brooklyn, NY 11235-2525
Phone: 718-332-8336
E-mail: wcfodogs@aol.com
Web site: www.worldcaninefreestyle.org

Further Reading

Aloff, Brenda. *Canine Body Language, a Photographic Guide*. Wenatchee, Wash.: Dogwise Publishing, 2005.

Bertilsson, Eva, and Emelie Johnson-Vegh. *Agility Right From The Start*. Waltham, Mass.: Sunshine Books, 2010.

Dennison, Pamela. *Click Your Way To Rally Obedience*. Loveland, Colo.: Alpine Publishing, 2006.

Gewirtz, Elaine. *Fetch This Book! Train Your Dog to Do Almost Anything*. Pittsburgh: Eldorado Ink, 2010.

Green, Peter, and Mario Migliorini. *New Secrets of Show Dog Handling*. Loveland, Colo.: Alpine Publishing, 2002.

Handler, Barbara. *Successful Obedience Handling*, 2nd ed. Loveland, Colo.: Alpine Publishing, 2003.

Hoffman, Gary. *Hiking With Your Dog*. 3rd ed. La Crescenta, Calif.: Mountain 'N Air Books, 2002.

Jones, Deb. *Click Here For a Well-Trained Dog*. Franklin, NY: Howln Moon, 2002.

Koshar, Claire. *A Guide To Dog Sports*. Wilsonville, Ore.: Doral Publishing, 2002.

McDevitt, Leslie. *Control Unleashed—Creating a Focused and Confident Dog*. South Hadley, Mass.: Clean Run Productions, 2007.

Olson, Lew. *Raw and Natural Nutrition For Dogs*. Berkeley, Calif.: North Atlantic Books, 2010.

Pitcairn, Richard, and Susan Pitcairn. *Dr. Pitcairn's Complete Guide To Natural Health For Dogs & Cats*. 3rd ed. Emmaus, Pa.: Rodale, 2005

Putney, William W., DVM. *Always Faithful: A Memoir of the Marine Dogs of WWII*. Dulles, Va.: Brassey's Inc., 2003.

Segal, Monica. *Deciphering Dog Food Labels—A Guide To Buying a Better Commercial Food*. Toronto: Doggie Diner, Inc., 2008.

Internet Resources

www.dpca.org

The Website of the Doberman Pinscher Club of America, the AKC parent club for the breed.

www.dpcarescue.com

This Doberman Pinscher breed rescue page provides resources to help Dobermans find new homes.

www.healthypet.com

The pet owner's website of the American Animal Hospital Association has lists of accredited veterinary hospitals in every state, along with up-to-date pet health info.

www.akc.org/breeds/doberman_pinscher

The American Kennel Club's breed standard for Doberman Pinschers is available at this Web site.

www.thekennelclub.org.uk/item/48

The Kennel Club of the United Kingdom posts its breed standard for Dobermanns at this Web site.

http://clickertraining.com/

Karen Pryor Clicker Training is an educational resource with information and how-to tips about clicker training, a form of operant conditioning that is both effective and enjoyable.

http://westminsterkennelclub.org

This Web site, sponsored by the Westminster Kennel Club, includes details about the Westminster Dog Show, as well as breed information and showmanship videos.

http://www.hsus.org

The official Web site for the Humane Society of the United States offers valuable information about pet adoption and pet issues.

http://www.aspca.org

The Web site of the American Society for the Prevention of Cruelty to Animals provides expert advice on pet care, animal behavior, and other pet-related topics.

Index

adoption, 34–36
aggression, 24, 29
    See also personality
agility trials, 86–88
airplane rides, 73–74
American Animal Hospital Association
    (AAHA), 52, 56
American Kennel Club (AKC), 12, 17,
    80–83
        Canine Good Citizen (CGC) test,
        90–91
appearance, *8*, 9, 19–21
automobile trips, 73
average life expectancy, 92

baby gate, use of, 40
bad breath, 96
barking, 28–29, 71, **97**
bathing. *See* grooming
behavior. *See* socialization
biting, 24
        See also socialization
bloat, 43, 60–62
bloat and torsion (Gastric Dilation
    Volvulus), 60–61
boarding kennels, 75
bordetella, 56–57
breed, selecting the right, 7
breed history, 16–21
breed standard, 17–21
breeders, 32–34
brushes, 45, *46*
buying a Doberman Pinscher, 32–34

canine adenovirus-2, 56
Canine Good Citizen (CGC) test, 90–91

Centers for Disease Control, 24
cervical spondylopathy. *See* Wobbler's
    Syndrome
chew toys. *See* toys
choosing the right breed, 7
coat care. *See* grooming
cognitive development, 44–45
collar tags, *22*, 24–25
collars, choosing, 40
colors, 20–21
commands, basic obedience, 77–80
competitions, 11, 31, 37
        agility trials, 86–88
        conformation shows, 19, 35, 80–83
        obedience trials, 35, 83–85
        Rally, 85–86
        tracking, 11, 31
conformation shows, 19, 35, 80–83
crates and crate training, 39–40
cropping. *See* tail docking and ear crop-
    ping

death, dealing with, 97–99
dental care, 48
diet. *See* food and diet
distemper, 56
DNA as means of identification, 24–25
Doberman Pinscher Club of America
    (DPCA), 18, *19*, 32–33
Doberman Pinschers
    from 6 months to 2 years, 65–75
    average life expectancy, 92
    breed history, 16–17
    breed standard, 12, 17–21
    choosing of, as pets, 30–37
    cognitive development, 44–45

Numbers in *bold italics* refer to captions.

costs of ownership of, 13–15, 81
dealing with death of, 97–99
exercise, 9–10, 13
health issues, 51–64, 93, 94, 96–97
housetraining, 39–40, 49–50
intelligence of, 9, *89*
and kids, 39
and other animals, 44–45, 54
personality of, *8*, 9, *13*, 31, 36–37, 91
physical appearance, *8*, 9, 19–21
popularity of, *8*, 9, 17
as puppies, 38–50, 54–55, 76
reasons for choosing, 9–15
roles of, 10–11, 18, 31, 88–90
as senior dogs, 92–99
training of, 10, 11, 13, 15, 40–41, 45, 76–91
Dobermann, Karl Friedrich Louis, 16, 17
docking. *See* tail docking and ear cropping
domestication of dogs, 6
dysplasia, 33, 54, 58–59

ear cropping. *See* tail docking and ear cropping
endocrine disorders, 66
euthanasia, 99
exercise, 69–70
play as, *44*
senior dogs, 94, *95*
exocrine pancreatic insufficiency (EPI), 58
external parasites (fleas and ticks), 63–64

fleas, 63–64
food and diet
adult nutrition, 43, 65–68
correct weight, 66–67
costs of ownership, 14
gulping air, 62
puppy nutrition, 42–44

selecting proper bowls, *41*
senior nutrition, 93

Gastric Dilation Volvulus. *See* bloat
gender as factor in selection, 30–31
Germany, 12, 16–17
grooming, 45–47, *46*
for conformation shows, 48, 80
costs of ownership, 15
supplies, 45, 46, 48
See also dental care; nail care

health issues, 51–64
bad breath, 96
bloat, 43, 60–62
dental care, 48
endocrine disorders, 66
exocrine pancreatic insufficiency (EPI), 58
gulping air, 62
hip dysplasia, 58–59
incontinence, 97
panosteitis, 59
parasites, 62–64
of senior dogs, 93, 94, 96–97
spaying and neutering, 26–27, 31
vaccinations, 29, 55–58
von Willebrand's Disease (vWD), 59
weight, 66–67, 93
when to visit the veterinarian, 68
Wobbler's Syndrome, 59–60
heartworms, 62–63
hip dysplasia, 58–59
home, dog-proofing the, 38–39
household rules, 28, 50
housetraining, 39–40, 49–50
See also training
Humane Society of the United States (HSUS), 26

identification, *22*, 24–26
incontinence, 97
insurance, pet, 27–28
intelligence, 9, *89*

"kennel cough," 56–57

leash laws, 28–29
leashes and leash training, *23*, 40–41
legal issues, 22–23, 28–29
    leash laws, 28–29
    liability, 24, 29
    licensing, 23
    nuisance laws, 28–29
    rabies vaccinations, 29
leptospirosis, 57
liability issues, 24, 29
licensing, 23
Lyme disease, 57

microchips, 26

nail care, 47–48, 80
National Association of Professional Pet
    Sitters (NAPPS), 75
neutering, 26–27, 31
nuisance laws, 28–29
nutrition. *See* food and diet

obedience training. *See* training
obedience trials, 35, 83–85
older dogs. *See* senior dogs
orthopedic disorders. *See* dysplasia
Orthopedic Foundations for Animals
    (OFA), 59
ownership, dog
    choosing a veterinarian, 51–53
    choosing your Doberman Pinscher,
        30–37
    cleaning up after, 28
    costs of ownership, 13–15, 81
    home environment, 38–42
    household rules, 28, 50
    identification, *22*, 24–26
    legal issues, 28–29
    paperwork, 33, 37, 54, 74
    pet insurance, 27–28
    responsibilities of, 22–29
    spaying and neutering, 26–27, 31

    supplies needed, 39–41
    training as a responsibility, 7
    traveling with a dog, 24–25, 72–74

panosteitis, 59
parainfluenza, 57–58
parasites (internal and external), 54,
    62–64
parvovirus, 56
personality, *8*, 9, *13*, 31, 36–37
    aggression, 24, 29
    changes in senior dogs, **97**
    impact of gender on, 31
    Temperament Test, 91
pet insurance, 27–28
pet sitters, 74–75
Pet Sitters International (PSI), 75
physical characteristics, 8, 9, 19–21
police dogs, 11, **89**
potty bell, 50
puppies, 38–50
    dog-proofing the home, 38–39
    first veterinary visit, 54–55
    housetraining, 39–40, 49–50
    preparations for, 38–41
    puppy nutrition, 42–44
    selection process, *32, 33*, 36–37
    socialization of, 44–45, 55
    supplies needed for, 39–41
    tail docking and ear cropping, 12, 21
    training of, 76
    See also Doberman Pinschers
puppy mills, 33

rabies vaccinations, 29, 56
Rally, 85–86
registration papers, 35, 37
rescue organizations, 34–36
roles of Doberman Pinschers, 10–11,
    18, 31, 88–90

search and rescue, 11
selecting the right Doberman Pinscher
    buying or adopting, 32–36

factors to consider, 30–32
senior dogs, 92–99
    dealing with death of, 97–99
service and therapy dogs, 11, 88–90
shelters, animal, 34–36
size, 20–21
socialization, 33, 70–72, 90
    Canine Good Citizen (CGC) test,
        90–91
    prevention of biting, 24
    of puppies, 44–45, 55
spaying, 26–27, 31
standard of perfection. *See* breed standard
    dard
supplies needed for a new puppy, 39–41

tail docking and ear cropping, 12, 21
tattoos, 25–26
temperament. *See* personality
Temperament Test, 91
therapy dogs, 88–90
Therapy Dogs International (TDI), *90*
ticks, 64
torsion. *See* bloat
toys, *14*, 15, 41, 48
tracking, 11, 31
training, 7, 15, 76–91
    agility trials, 86–88

basic obedience commands, 77–80
Canine Good Citizen (CGC) test,
    90–91
conformation shows, 19, 35, 80–83
costs of ownership, 15
housetraining, 39–40, 49–50
leash training, *23*, 40–41
at mealtimes, 84
obedience trials, 83–85
Puppy Kindergarten, 45
Rally, 85–86
search and rescue, 11
service and therapy dogs, 88–90
tracking, 11, 31
traveling with a dog, 24–25, 72–74
    leaving dog behind, 74–75

vaccinations, 29, 55–58
    See also health issues
veterinarians, 51–55, 68
    costs of ownership, 14
von Willebrand's Disease (vWD), 59

war, dogs of, 18
weight, keeping correct, 66–67, 93
Wobbler's Syndrome (cervical spondy-
    lopathy), 59–60
working dog, role as, 10–11, 18, 31, 88–90

Contributors

SEPTEMBER MORN is a professional dog trainer and freelance writer. September owns Dogs Love School, in Shelton, Washington, and currently shares her home and heart with Rottweilers and a miniature American Eskimo Dog. Her other books in Eldorado Ink's OUR BEST FRIENDS series include *The German Shepherd, The Golden Retriever*, and *The Pug.*

Senior Consulting Editor **GARY KORSGAARD, DVM,** has had a long and distinguished career in veterinary medicine. After graduating from The Ohio State University's College of Veterinary Medicine in 1963, he spent two years as a captain in the Veterinary Corps of the U.S. Army. During that time he attended the Walter Reed Army Institute of Research and became Chief of the Veterinary Division for the Sixth Army Medical Laboratory at the Presidio, San Francisco.

In 1968 Dr. Korsgaard founded the Monte Vista Veterinary Hospital in Concord, California, where he practiced for 32 years as a small animal veterinarian. He is a past president of the Contra Costa Veterinary Association, and was one of the founding members of the Contra Costa Veterinary Emergency Clinic, serving as president and board member of that hospital for nearly 30 years.

Dr. Korsgaard retired in 2000. He enjoys golf, hiking, international travel, and spending time with his wife Susan and their three children and four grandchildren.